Travel Light

How to Go Anywhere in the World
With Only One Suitcase
By

Joy Nyquist

Newjoy Press
4040 Piedmont Drive, Space 370
Highland, California 92346 USA

Travel Light
How to Go Anywhere in the World
With Only One Suitcase
by

Joy Nyquist

Published by:
Newjoy Press
4040 Piedmont Drive, Sp. 370
Highland, CA 92346 USA

Second Edition 2005
Copyright © 2001 by Joy Nyquist
First Edition 2001
Printed in the United States of America

Library of Congress Data

Nyquist, Joy
 Travel Light: How To Go Anywhere in the World With Only One Suitcase

 Includes bibliography and index

 1. Travel planning
 2. Travelers' health
 3. Travel safety
 5. Resources for travelers

ISBN 1-879899-25-6   **LCCN: pending**

DEDICATION

To my sister, Margaret

Thank you for making our travel
together so much fun.

TABLE OF CONTENTS

ABOUT THE AUTHOR

Traveling has been an exciting, lifelong avocation for author, Joy Nyquist. She has visited England, Scotland, Canada, Mexico, the Caribbean, and many states in the U.S., including Alaska and Hawaii. Her ambition is to see the rest of the world in the next few years.

Joy only recently began to put her ideas into books. Writing is her third career. She was a wife and mother for twelve years. After a divorce, she cared for her three children and went to college to become a registered nurse. She has been a nurse for more than 30 years, working in intensive care units, obstetrics and mental health. She has been a member of the International Society of Travel Medicine.

On the verge of retirement from nursing, she decided to pursue a long standing desire to be a writer. This is the second edition of her second nonfiction book. Her first book, *Travelers Health Handbook,* was written in 1993. It is being revised for a new edition..

DISCLAIMER

This book is designed to provide information about the subject matter covered. It is sold with the understanding that neither the author nor the publisher are engaged in presenting professional services through this book.

Every effort has been made to make this book as complete and accurate as possible. However, there may be mistakes both in typography and in content. This book should only be used as a general guide and not as the ultimate source of travel information.

The purpose of this book is to provide travel information and to entertain. The author and Newjoy Press shall have neither liability nor responsibility to any person or entity with respect to any loss or damage caused, or alleged to be caused, directly or indirectly by the information contained in this book.

If you do not wish to be bound by the above statements, you may return this book to the publisher for a full refund.

INTRODUCTION

8:20 a.m. The tour bus idles at the curb. The eager travelers inside are ready to leave for the day's adventures. Ripples of talk and laughter ebb and flow.

The passengers give quick glances at their watches, wondering a little about the delay. The bus was scheduled to leave at 8:00 a.m. The tour bus driver, usually a most congenial man, is sitting in the driver's seat with his back to the passengers.

Suddenly, the hotel door bursts open. A red-faced, sweating man and harried-looking woman loaded with large and small suitcases struggle out. Hanging from their shoulders and arms are assorted bags and cameras. Following them is a porter laden with more luggage.

With a small sigh, the driver gets out of the bus to load their baggage. (The tour guidelines clearly state that the tour staff is responsible for loading and unloading just one suitcase per person.) The embarrassed couple avoid other people's eyes as they get on the bus and sit down.

Twenty-five minutes after the scheduled departure, the driver guides the bus onto the road.

A man whispers to his companion, "What do they do with all that stuff? They are no better dressed or groomed than the rest of us on this tour."

Have you ever been part of a scenario like this? Maybe you were the embarrassed person! When you see yourself traveling, do you dream about the wonderful places you will see and the people you will meet? Chances are you *do not plan* to use precious travel time hauling, packing, and unpacking suitcases.

Did not plan. That's your clue. It may seem paradoxical, but the most carefree travel is *planned.* With the right strategy, you will spend your time enjoying the pleasures of traveling because the nitty-gritty details are out of your way in advance.

All the information you need for traveling light is at your disposal in this book. You will learn:

- How to obtain the travel documents you need
- How much time to allow for obtaining all the documents necessary before traveling overseas
- How to keep your home secure while you are away
- Simple tips to prevent damage to your home while you travel
- Where to find the insurance you need—including medical insurance
- How to protect your health while traveling ·
- Where to find competent medical help overseas.
- What kind of clothes and how much to pack to be comfortable and well dressed for all occasions
- How to pass through customs quickly with no hassles
- What kinds of luggage, purses, and carry-on bags to buy
- How to protect yourself and your possessions while traveling
- How to use the resources in this book to find more information
- How to use the extra copy of all the lists
- How to make traveling with children fun

Organization is an essential part of travel planning. At the end of each chapter you will find lists to help you keep track of everything you need to do and what to collect for your travel. *TIP: Save your lists and leave them at home when you travel. You will have an inventory of your belongings in case of loss or theft. Your lists from the trip will also help to make planning your next trip easier.*

Make your plans early. At least a week before your departure date, have all preparations completed. Stash everything you plan to take with you in one place where it is ready to be packed in your suitcase. I will show you how to do this in the next chapters.

With advance preparation for most contingencies completed, you are ready to relax and enjoy your travel.

The goal of this book is to help you achieve the maximum of enjoyment with the minimum of hassles.

Chapter One

TRAVEL DOCUMENTS

Passport

Your most important travel document is your passport. You should have it with you at all times during travel outside the United States.

Every citizen from birth on must have a valid passport when traveling outside the U.S.

All American citizens, native and naturalized, are eligible to apply for a U.S. passport. Those younger than 18 years pay less for their passport, valid for only five years. The adult passport is valid for ten years.

NOTE: Go to http://travel.state.gov or call 877-487-2778 for answers to questions on travel and passports from the U.S. State Department.

To apply for a new passport you will need. . .

1. **An application.** Form No. DS-11 is available at passport offices, federal and state courts, some probate courts, and larger U.S. post offices. Thirteen major cities have passport agencies. You can also download an application from the Internet at http://travel.state.gov.
2. **Proof of citizenship.** A certified copy of your birth certificate, a previous U.S. passport, or naturalization papers are the most common forms of proof. If you have none of

the above, check with agents at the acceptance office for documents that can be used in their place.

3. **Proof of identity.** The card or document must contain a signature and picture. Acceptable IDs include a valid driver's license, a government (federal, state, or municipal) identification card, a previous U.S. passport, or a Certificate of Naturalization or Citizenship.

4. **Two passport photographs.** The photos must be no more than six months old, depict a front-facing view of your head and neck, and be 2" by 2" in size. They can be either black-and-white or color, but must be taken against a plain white background. (Photo machine pictures are not acceptable.) Sign each picture on the back with your legal signature. It must be identical to your signature on the application. Many photographers will take the pictures for a fee. AAA members can obtain the photos through the club.

TIP: Buy extra pictures—one for each visa, two for an international driver's license, and two to four spares to have with you in case you lose your passport.

5 **Your Social Security number** must be provided or the IRS may impose a $500 penalty.

6. **A check, money order, or cashier's check for the fee.** At the time of this writing, the fee is $85 for a ten-year passport. You may pay by credit card, debit card, check, money order, or bank drafts. Make your check or money order payable to Passport Services. Post offices and passport agencies accept cash in the exact amount of the fee, but courts are not required to do so. Call in advance to find out the amount of the fee, acceptable methods of payment, and the hours of operation. Look for *Passports* in the U.S.

Government section of the phone book or go to the web site listed above.

Appear in person at a passport office if:
▸ You are applying for a passport for the first time.
▸ Your previous U.S. passport was lost, stolen, or damaged.
▸ Your previous U.S. passport was issued more than 15 years ago and has expired.
▸ Your previous passport was issued when you were under 16 years of age and has expired.
▸ Your name has changed since your passport was issued and you do not have a legal document formally changing your name.
▸ You are a minor 14 years of age or older.

How long does it take?
It can take six weeks or longer to receive a passport in the mail. Check on the status of your passport application by calling the National Passport Information Center. Call 1-877-487-2778. Live operators available on weekdays 8 am to 8 pm EST. Automated service available 24/7. E-mail service is available. They respond within 24 hours during normal business weekday hours. Send inquiries to *npic@state.gov*

Passport renewal
1. Obtain an application (form No. DS82) from a passport agency or the internet at http://travel.state.gov.
2. Return the completed form, your old passport, the fee (check, money order, or cashier's check) and two *new* photos (see photo requirements above) to the nearest passport agency or mail to: National Passport Center, P.O. Box 371971, Pittsburgh, PA 15250-1971. Mail the materials in a padded bag. (Not essential but the bag offers protection

against mutilation in transit.) Your old passport will be returned to you with the new passport.

3. If your name has changed since you acquired your first passport, you must include a *certified* copy of the court order, divorce decree, or marriage certificate specifying another name for you to use. (They will not accept photocopies.)

4. You can renew your passport in person or by mail. However, if your old passport is mutilated, altered, damaged, or expired more than two years ago, you must apply in person.

5. Applications are processed according to the departure date shown on the application.

Fast passports

If you have an emergency and need a passport within five working days, apply in person at the nearest passport agency.

In addition to all the required items listed above, bring your travel tickets and itinerary. You must pay a $30 expediting fee in addition to the regular fee.

Get your passport early

Apply for a passport several months before your travel, especially if you need visas. When your passport arrives in the mail, check it carefully for accuracy *before* you sign it. If there is an error, you must send it back to be corrected. If you make alterations to your passport, you render it invalid. In effect, an altered passport is not legally a passport at all!

Be sure your address appears on your passport.

Make two copies of your passport on a photocopier. Carry the original with you. Keep one copy in the hotel's or ship's safe with your other valuables. (Safeguarding the copies of your passport is very important. You don't want someone else to use it to apply for a passport in your name). Leave the second copy with your contact person at home.

If your passport is lost or stolen, call the local police and the nearest U.S. consulate or embassy *immediately!* Since 9/11 the process of getting a new passport while traveling is somewhat complicated. You must submit Form DS-64 along with a copy of the passport, legal identification, and two spare photos to the nearest U.S. Embassy or Consulate. The replacement process may take a few days as they check your information.

TIP: Your passport is the most valuable piece of identification you own. When you are in a foreign country without a passport, you are a tourist with no country. American passports are valuable commodities for thieves and terrorists. Consider making or buying a lightweight pouch to wear around your neck or waist, under your clothing. You can purchase such a pouch at luggage, camping, and travel stores (see Resource Section).

Traveling in Canada, Central America, South America, and some Caribbean countries does not require a passport, but it is a good idea to carry yours with you. It is the most reliable proof of citizenship.

Experienced travelers always take a passport. Other acceptable documents include certified copies of birth or naturalization certificates. A driver's license proves identity, not citizenship.

Some countries require your passport to be valid six months or longer beyond the conclusion of your travel. If your passport will expire before the required time, you must apply for a new one. Check with the consulates of the countries you plan to visit for their requirements.

Visas

A visa, in addition to a passport, is required for entry into some countries. The list of countries requiring a visa is decreasing but be sure to check. Early in your travel planning, find out the current requirements of each country you plan to visit and to travel through.

On the internet, go to the U.S. State Department site *www.travel.state.gov*. Click on Travel Warnings and Consular Information. At the bottom of the page, select the first letter of the country for which you'd like information. Then select the country to receive detailed information.

Not on the internet? Travel agents may have the information or you can call the embassy or consulate of the country you plan to visit or travel through. Find them in the white pages of the phone book or through directory information.

NOTE: You may not be staying in a country requiring a visa, but if you will be traveling through such a country by train, bus, or car, you need a visa. Plane travel is not a problem unless you will be landing in the country requiring a visa. This includes landing to make connecting flights if you have to go through their airport.

You may also send for a booklet from the U.S. State Department called *Foreign Entry Requirements (see Resource Section)*

Travel agencies and tour companies may have the information. Making a few phone calls on your own is best so you have first hand, current information.

When you call an embassy or consulate for visa information and find out you need one, ask them to send (via fax or the internet if possible) you an application. Also ask for the days and times you can apply, the fee and the form of payment they will accept.

For the fastest processing of visas, pick up the application and deliver your completed application in person at the embassy or consulate during the times and days they designate. Take the following items:
1. Your passport.
2. The fee in the form required.
3. Your photographs (see passport photo requirements).
4. A fully completed application.
5. Any other identification or documents required by the country.

Depending on the country and its requirements, visa processing can vary from an hour to several weeks.

You may be able to apply for a visa by mail. Call each embassy for the exact requirements and an application. Send the documents required. These usually include your passport, the complete application, and the fee in the form they require. Send everything to the embassy by certified, overnight mail.

NOTE: *It is extremely important to enclose a self-addressed envelope and enough postage so your passport and visa can be sent back to you by certified, overnight mail.*

Each visa may take several weeks, especially if you use the mail. Since you must send your passport with each application, be sure you allow enough time.

Health requirements.
Some countries require an International Certificate of Vaccination for yellow fever.

Some countries require HIV testing. Check with CDC or the countries' embassy or consulate.

Prophylactic medication for select diseases are advised by the CDC before traveling to some countries.

Obtain current health information from the Center for Disease Control. For detailed, current data, call 1-877-394-8747 or go to their web site, *www.cdc.gov.*
See Chapter Six for more health care information.

International Driver's License

You will need a current, valid driver's license and two photographs, 2" by 2". The AAA and other auto clubs can issue the license or ask a travel agent to help you. You must have a valid U.S. driver's license to qualify for an IDL. Your IDL will come with pages of translations you can use to as a communication tool in foreign countries.

Proof of solvency

Some countries require proof you can support yourself while in their country. They may require a statement from your bank and/or funds on deposit in their country.

Other countries want to know if you can afford to leave the country when your visit is over. Showing your return ticket is usually sufficient proof. Still, it pays to check the requirements for each country you plan to visit. You can find the exact information you need on http://travel.state.gov

Many countries charge for exit stamps when you are leaving. Be sure to know the amount and plan for it in your travel budget.

Your travel agent should know—or be able to find out for you—the current requirements. You can also ask each country's tourist offices. If you are going on a tour or cruise, the details will usually be taken care of for you by the tour or cruise company. Ask them if this service is part of the package. Independent travelers will need to obtain the information themselves. A few phone calls may be all it takes to be prepared and avoid problems.

RailEurope and Britrail pass

Trains in Britain and continental Europe are fast, comfortable, and usually on time. Sightseeing by rail is an excellent way to see countries. You can save a considerable amount of money by buying passes *before you leave home.* You *cannot* buy them in Britain or continental Europe.

Three to four months in advance of your travel, request an application and instructions from your travel agent or directly from RailEurope *(see Resource Section).* Complete the application as instructed and send it in with your fee.

Before sending the application and fee, make a copy of the application. Obtain an address and phone number to call if you do not receive your passes within six to eight weeks.

RailEurope handles passes and reservations for Britrail.

Car rental

Many options are available from travel agencies, auto clubs, and car rental companies. A most important factor is to reserve early, especially if you are going to travel during peak seasons and/or need a car with an automatic transmission.

Gasoline prices are very high in Europe and Asia. When you reserve your car, ask for gasoline prices at your destination so you can estimate your costs.

Don't forget to buy insurance and obtain a copy of the highway code of the countries where you will be driving.

For more tips, see Chapter Four.

Cash

Before you travel, exchange a couple of days supply of your country's money for the currency of the first country you will be visiting. You can exchange money at most large international banks. Having a little local money will enable you to pay for taxis, a meal, and incidentals while you check out the local exchange rate. If you can't exchange before your travel, use the airport exchange machines when you arrive.

If you are traveling to several countries, exchange money in each country as you need it. Using ATMs makes it easy. ATMs and banks will usually give you the lowest exchange rates.

Change any foreign currency back to your country's currency before you leave a foreign country.

Don't carry much cash. Keep most of what you do carry in the travel pouch with your passport.

NOTE: Most people who travel plan to spend a certain amount of money for the trip. When you decide the sum you want to spend, calculate your fixed costs such as airline fare, tour services, meals, other transportation, rental cars, hotels, etc. If you are not sure about the cost of something, have your travel agent help you make an estimate. Be generous in your fixed estimates. After deducting your fixed costs, the amount left can be divided by the number of days you will be traveling. You will know exactly how much you can spend and still stay within your budget.

Credit cards

The most widely accepted credit cards overseas are MasterCard, Visa, American Express, and Diner's Club.

Make two copies of your card numbers and the addresses, phone numbers, and procedures for reporting lost or stolen cards.

Keep one copy of the information in your luggage separate from the cards. Leave the other copy with your contact person back home.

Notify your credit card company that you will be traveling abroad and may have more than usual activity on your card. If you don't, they may arbitrarily cut you off from using the card. Also, some credit card companies are charging an extra fee on overseas use of their card. This may be two percent or more. Check with your cardholder for information about this fee.

TIP: Don't take all your credit cards with you. Travel experts advise taking only one or two cards, at least one of which you can use in an ATM. ATMs are widely available and you can easily obtain local currency though them.

Travelers checks

Travelers' checks are usually not the best way to take money with you when you travel. Many places charge an extra fee to cash the checks and some places will not take them at all. If you do take them, have them exchanged for cash at a bank or exchange machine as you need them. However, even banks will charge you a fee for the exchange.

▸ Take time to sign all the checks when you buy them.
▸ Keep most of the checks in the hotel or cruise ship safe. Carry on your person only what you will use for the day.
▸ Make two copies of a list of the travelers' check numbers. Carry one copy of the list in your luggage separate from the checks. Leave one list at home with a trusted relative or friend. Each day, on your copy, cross off the checks you use. You will have a current list of checks in case they are lost or stolen. Replacement will be quick and easy.
▸ Purchase most of your checks in the $20 denomination. They are easier to cash.
▸ Stick to internationally recognized companies when you buy your checks.
▸ Members of AAA, other auto clubs, and some banks allow you to buy travelers' checks without paying a fee.

Automatic Teller Machines (ATM)

ATMs are found in most parts of the world. It is easy to use your card to exchange dollars for the currency of the country. Keep a running total of how much you have available and how much you have spent. This is an easy way to carry only the cash you need for each day. However, observe the following precautions:

▸ Be careful no one can see you enter your PIN. Use your body to shield the ATM machine from the view of others.

▸ When you are as sure as possible you are unobserved, quickly tuck your money away.

▸ Avoid ATMs at night, especially if you are alone.

▸ In third world countries, eastern Europe, and Italy, use banks to exchange money instead of ATMs.

Proof of prior possession

Before taking expensive jewelry, cameras, computers, watches, furs, and other valuable items out of the country, you must secure proof you owned them before you began your travel. The best proof is the original receipt for each item. Insurance policies and jewelers' appraisals are acceptable. If you do not have any of the above proofs, take the item to a customs office for registration before you travel.

Take color pictures of your valuables so you won't have to try to describe them if they are lost or stolen.

TIP: Savvy travelers don't usually take valuables with them. Carry an inexpensive camera and watch. Leave jewels and furs at home.

Personal checks

They are rarely accepted. The hassle is not worth it. Leave them home.

Phone cards

You can buy prepaid phone cards in the U.S., buy cards in many European countries, or use your calling card. Discuss options with a travel agent or phone company.

Other documents you need to take with you are named on the following list.

Travel Document List

☐ Passports

☐ Name_____No. _____

☐ Name_____No _____

☐ Name_____No. _____

☐ Name_____No. _____

☐ Name_____No. _____

☐ Visas

    ☐ _____

    ☐ _____

    ☐ _____

    ☐ _____

    ☐ _____

☐ Copies of Passports/Visas

☐ International Driver's License

☐ Proof of Solvency

☐ RailEurope Pass

☐ Britrail Pass

☐ Rental Car Agent _____

☐ Rental Car Confirmation No _____

☐ Travelers' Checks

- ☐ List of travelers' check numbers (2 copies)
- ☐ Exchanged Cash
- ☐ Credit/ATM cards
- ☐ Visa
  - ☐ MasterCard
  - ☐ American Express
  - ☐ Diner's Club
- ☐ Proof of Prior Possession

  Item _____

  Item _____

  Item _____
- ☐ Airline Tickets
- ☐ Tour Documents
- ☐ Cruise Documents
- ☐ Confirmation Numbers for Hotel   _____
- ☐ Currency Converter
- ☐ Guidebooks/Maps
- ☐ Travel Agent's Phone No.   _____
- ☐ Itinerary
- ☐ Itinerary Copy to Relatives/contact Person
- ☐ Amount Allotted for Each Day $ _____
- ☐ Phone Cards

Chapter Two

INSURANCE

Most travel is free of major incidents and you return home with happy memories. However, the risk of illness, accident, or another unforeseen event is present when you travel just as it is when you are at home. You need insurance. Your present policies may already cover you but it pays to check. Talk to your insurance agents about what your health insurance and auto insurance will cover while you travel.

In this chapter, you will learn what to ask the agent so you will travel well informed about your coverage.

As you travel, with your insurance policy keep the addresses, phone numbers, fax numbers, agent's name, policy numbers and specific information about filing a claim.

Health and life insurance

Your medical insurance may cover you while you travel. Review your policy with your carrier to be sure. Inexpensive travelers' insurance policies are available to cover anything your medical insurance does not.

Medicare will not cover you while you are abroad except for some special circumstances in Mexico and Canada. If Medicare is your only health insurance, you will need a travel policy.

Many insurers will not pay for medically required evacuation nor for getting your body home should you die overseas. Know if your policy covers these situations.

Find out if your regular insurer or the travel insurer will pay the overseas providers of care directly or if you will have to cover the cost and be reimbursed later. Obtain from them any forms or identification you will need. Take the agent's and the claims department's phone and fax numbers with you.

In the event you have to pay up front and be reimbursed later, arrange for a source of funds you can use to pay for any medical care.

Some policies have age restrictions and most refuse to cover preexisting conditions. Some will allow a waiver of restrictions if a doctor writes a letter stating you are unlikely to need treatment while traveling.

Glasses, contact lenses, and hearing aids are seldom covered. Dental care most often includes accidental injury only. A few policies include relief of dental pain.

You can obtain travel insurance from AAA and American Express. Following is a web site for travelers' insurance.

TIP: Http://InsureMyTrip.com bills itself as "The Travel Insurance Comparison Site." You can get quotes from numerous travel insurance companies, compare exactly what features they offer, and their prices. You can also check the A.M. Best ratings for each company to be sure you are buying from a financially stable insurer.

Overseas assistance for U. S. Citizens

When you travel independently, you can get help from American Embassies and Consulates; the Overseas Citizen Services or American Express (members only).

The Overseas Citizen Services deals with emergencies involving individual Americans abroad such as, death, sickness, destitution, accidents or arrest. Working with embassies and consulates, the center is the link between the citizens in distress and their families in the U.S. When calling from the United States, their phone number is 888-407-4747, twenty-four hours a day, seven days a week. If you call from overseas, the phone number is 317-472-2328.

Trip cancellation or interruption insurance

Most tour and cruise companies include this type of insurance as a part of the package when you book with them. If the company must cancel or interrupt a tour or cruise for reasons such as weather, damaged equipment, political turmoil, etc., you will get your money back. Read your documents and review them with your travel agent before you purchase any additional insurance.

Trip cancellation and interruption insurance usually won't cover you if you change your mind about taking the trip after paying for it. The insurance *will* reimburse you for what you lose when you have sickness, injury and other specified emergencies. The insurance will also reimburse you (or your heirs) in case of your death, the death of your travel companion or members of your immediate family.

Before you buy, be sure the policy includes:

▸ Non-refundable deposits coverage.
▸ Flight cancellation charges.
▸ Reimbursement for anything a bankrupt tour operator or airline cannot repay.
▸ Airfare for you to return home or catch up with your group if illness or injury delays you.
▸ Reimbursement for hotel rooms and meals you must have if there is a delay or change of plans due to no fault of yours.

TIP: On escorted tours a travel assistance policy may be a part of the tour package and the tour guide will help with many emergencies. However, it pays to check. Cruise ships must have medical personnel on board. The crew is available to help you with non-medical problems.

Lost, stolen or damaged luggage

Airlines are required to reimburse you for lost or damaged luggage. The current reimbursement for lost luggage is $2,500. The airlines also will pay for repairs to damaged luggage. This may be negotiable depending on damage. Ask your airline representative or your travel agent about airlines' limits and requirements. Find out if they will replace toiletries and basic clothing if luggage is delayed or lost for more than a day.

NOTE: Avoid the inconvenience of having to replace lost or delayed necessities by packing a change of clothing, toiletries, medication, and your valuables in your carry-on bag.

Check out the insurance your credit card company includes if you charge airline tickets, tours or hotel rooms.

Check your homeowner's or renter's policy. It may include reimbursement for depreciated cost of lost or stolen effects taken with you and/or repair of damaged items. Because of the high risk of theft, furs, jewelry, and expensive photography equipment are excluded from most homeowner and travel policies

TIP: The lists you make when you follow the guidelines in this book will be helpful in proving what is lost.

Car insurance—foreign travel

If you are planning to drive in foreign countries, be aware that each country has it own set of rules. Check with your travel agent, car rental agency or on the internet for the highway code of the countries where you plan to drive. Some countries have a

Highway Code available from their tourist bureau. Britain is one of them.

Rental car companies will usually give you information about the insurance requirements for their car when you arrange for the rental. If they don't give you detailed information and a policy, be sure to ask for it.

Travel in Canada

Travel into Canada has become more restrictive since 9/11. Motorists visiting Canada from the U.S. can be assured of coverage via their existing car insurance policies if their company has agreed with Canadian authorities to provide such coverage. No amendment to your insurance policy is necessary. However, you will need obtain a yellow *Non-Resident Inter-Province Motor Vehicle Liability Insurance Card* from your insurance agent.

The card will show your insurance company is willing to meet the minimum financial responsibility requirements of Canada, thus eliminating the possibility your car will be impounded or your driving privileges suspended in the event of an accident. Keep the card in your vehicle at all times.

The car registration must be in your name. If you drive another person's vehicle, you need a letter from the owner giving you permission to cross an international border with their vehicle.

Be aware of the rules of the road in each province.

Travel in Mexico

You must purchase special Mexican auto insurance before leaving the U.S. If you don't have the proper insurance and become involved in an accident, your car will be confiscated. You may end up in jail even if the accident is clearly not your fault. In Mexico, under Napoleonic law, you are presumed guilty and must prove your innocence in any legal situation.

Mexican insurance companies are found in many U.S. cities near the border and on the internet at *www.mexonline.com.*

Proper protection will be provided by buying the short-term *Special Automobile Policy for Tourists.* Cost will vary depending upon the places you go, the time you will spend in Mexico, the value of your car, and how much coverage you want. Make sure you get a listing of the agents and the adjuster representing the Mexican company. Keep this information with your policy, easily accessible while you drive in Mexico.

If you will be traveling more than 20 miles from the border, it is important to have an international credit card and passport. Check on the *www.mexonline.com* site or at the nearest Mexican consulate.

Car insurance for travel in U.S.A.

Each state has its own rules of the road. However, every state requires auto insurance. Check with tourist bureaus of each state in which you plan to drive for their driving laws and insurance requirements.

Insurance Checklist

☐ Health insurance policy # _____

☐ Company _____

☐ Agent's name _____

☐ Phone No. _____

☐ Fax No. _____

Trip cancellation or interruption insurance to include:

  ☐ Nonrefundable deposits

  ☐ Flight Cancellation charges

  ☐ Reimbursement for bankrupt tour operator

  ☐ Reimbursement for what airline can't repay.

  ☐ Airfare for a return home or catch up with group

  ☐ Reimbursement for hotel rooms and meals if a delay or change of plans is not your fault.

  ☐ Lost, stolen or damaged luggage and/or other loss

Credit card company's insurance for:

☐ Airline tickets

☐ Tours

☐ Hotel rooms

☐ Purchased items

Car Insurance

☐ Company _____

☐ Policy Number _____

☐ Agent _____

☐ Claim forms or procedures for filing claim

☐ Phone number_____

☐ Fax Number _____

Chapter Three

HOME PREPARATION AND SAFETY

Travel preparations aren't just about what you will take and do while traveling. Safeguarding your home and its contents while you are away is important, too. Ensure your peace of mind with common sense arrangements you make *before* your travel for the safety of your home while you travel.

Contact person

First and foremost, ask a trusted person to be the eyes and ears around your home while you are gone.

▸ Give him or her a set of keys for your home, car, garage and storage areas.

▸ Be sure he or she knows the name of your attorney, (if you have one) and where you keep your will and other important papers.

▸ Give him or her names of your relatives to be notified in case of an emergency. Also give your relatives the name, address and phone number of the contact person.

▸ If your contact person or your relatives don't live in your neighborhood, furnish a list of your neighbors and your landlord to them..

▸ Provide a detailed itinerary of your trip.

Arrange to phone the helping person at regular intervals throughout your absence if possible. Ask them to check your premises two or three times a week.

Inform your trusted neighbors that you will be gone and how long. Give them the name and phone number of the person who will be taking care of your property. Ask them to accept delivery of any packages from UPS or other delivery services and to call the police if they see any suspicious activity.

If you live in an apartment or condo, consider notifying the manager you will be gone.

Locks for maximum protection

Inspect the locks on windows, doors, garage and storage buildings. The maximum security door lock is the double-cylinder deadbolt. All dead bolts should have a bolt extending at least one inch when locked; a cylinder guard ring of hardened steel; and a hardened steel insert or bearing within the bolt to prevent someone from sawing through the bolt.

If glass is within 40" of the locking hardware, a double cylinder dead bolt, operated only by a key inside and out, is suggested by safety experts

WARNING: When at home, leave the key in or near the lock for quick exit in an emergency such as fire.

Sliding glass doors are a favorite means of entry for burglars since they are usually easy to force open. Take away some of the ease of entry by placing a heavy wooden dowel in the lower track of the door. Be sure it fits snugly in the track and is the entire width of the track.

To prevent the door from being lifted out of its track, put two or three sheet metal screws into the track above the sliding door. They should protrude so the top of the closing door just clears them.

Other locking methods for sliding doors are available. However, the above methods are effective and easy.

Overhead garage doors should be secured by padlocking both sides on the outside. Quality padlocks have laminated or extruded cases; minimum 9/32" hardened steel shackle; double lock mechanism, heel and toe; five pin tumbler and key retaining feature. Use quality hasps with unexposed screws. Unplug your automatic garage door opener.

Lock all doors and windows in the home, garage and storage buildings before you leave. Securely lock all gates.

Prepare your home for your absence

▸ Use a timer or photoelectric cell to automatically turn outside lights on at dusk and off at dawn. Install them now so anyone "casing" the neighborhood will see that you are home while the lights are working. They will be less likely to notice something different when you are gone.

▸ Inside the house, plug in two or more appliance timers to simulate the pattern of lights going on and off as they do when you are home.

▸ Cancel your newspaper delivery. Burglars and vandals love to see piled up newspapers in front of a house. It is like an "open sesame" for them.

▸ Have your mail held at the post office. They will hold mail for 30 days. If you are going to be away longer than that, you must arrange to have your mail picked up for you.

▸ Arrange for your yard maintenance while you are gone. Have someone water your lawn and plants, mow your grass or remove snow. Trim shrubs that can conceal someone sneaking around the house.

- Trim trees that allow access to a second story of your house. Lock ladders away so no one has access to them.
- Inside the house, unplug appliances. Unplug your computer, television, microwave, etc. An electrical storm or short while you are gone can destroy your computer and any other electronic equipment. Keep the lamps that will light automatically plugged in.
- Give away or throw away all perishable food in your refrigerator. Turn the thermostat to a low setting.
- Turn your water heater off or down to the lowest setting. Turning it off is best. If you decide to turn off the heater, shut off the water supply also.
- Turn off the water supply to your washer, ice-maker, coolers and any other appliances with a water hose. The damage to your house by water from a broken hose can be devastating.

A friend of mine was gone for the day from her house. In her absence, the hose to the washer broke. The water caused $18,000 worth of damage in just a few hours!

- Maintain an up-to-date list of serial numbered property. Inscribe an identifying number (driver's license number or last four digits of social security number) on other valuables.
- Write out an accurate description and take photographs of items such as jewelry or furs that cannot be marked
- Have checks due to you while you are gone sent directly to your bank for deposit. This is not only for protection, it may help to have the extra money available in your account for emergencies or just for that special item you can't resist.
- Take care of your pets. Arrange for a kennel, a friend or relative to provide care while you are gone. Take your pet to

the place where they will be staying for a few times to visit before you leave them. Hopefully, they won't be distressed when you drop them off.

‣ Cancel any standing appointments such as with the hairdresser.

‣ Don't leave a message on your phone that will tell people you are gone. Check your messages frequently while you are away or have someone do it for you.

TIP: As you call people and businesses, make a list to leave by the phone. When you return, you won't have to look up numbers to restart your services.

Security Systems

Consider installing a security system connected to a central office especially if you have highly valuable items in your home. The police or representative of the company will respond when the security alarm sounds.

If a complete security system is too expensive for you, install a house system that sounds a loud, persistent noise. Be sure to tell your neighbors about your system so they will call the police when it sounds. Don't forget to tell them how to turn it off!

Home Safety List

☐ Contact person _____

   Address   _____

   City, State, Zip   _____

   Phone   _____

   E-mail   _____

☐ Itinerary to contact person. Include the names of ships or hotels and their phone numbers.

Keys to contact person:
☐ Home
☐ Garage
☐ Car
☐ Storage area
☐ Safe deposit box
☐ Post Office Box
☐ _____

Give neighbors:
☐ The name of your contact person
☐ Permission to accept packages
☐ Instructions for turning off any alarms
☐ Ask them to call police if they see any suspicious activity.

Home checklist

- ☐ Secure and lock sliding glass doors
- ☐ Lock doors with a dead bolt.
- ☐ Close and lock all windows
- ☐ Lock garage and turn off automatic opener
- ☐ Lock storage building
- ☐ Install security system
- ☐ Install alarms
- ☐ Activate an outside light timer now.
- ☐ Activate appliance timers on inside lamps.
- ☐ Cancel newspaper
- ☐ Place hold on mail
- ☐ Arrange for yard maintenance
- ☐ Unplug appliances
- ☐ Empty refrigerator - turn off or to low setting.
- ☐ Turn off water heaters
- ☐ Turn off all faucets
- ☐ List serial numbered property
- ☐ Photograph valuable items
- ☐ Arrange for direct deposit of checks
- ☐ Arrange for pet care
- ☐ Reschedule standing appointments
- ☐ Clear flammable materials from the house and garage.

Chapter Four

TRAVEL SAFETY

Travel safety has been a critical concern of knowledgeable travelers since the terrorist attacks of 9/11/01 in the United States and the vicious attacks on innocent persons in Spain in March of 2004. A moderate dose of paranoia can be helpful when you travel. Follow safety rules to the letter. Be aware of what is going on around you in airports, train stations, and other public places. Don't hesitate to report unusual behavior or packages. Persons planning criminal acts count on the apathy of the public.

The Transportation Security Administration was formed to help travelers be prepared for their journeys.

See *www.tsatraveltips.us* and *www.airsafe.com* for detailed safety information.

Basic advice for air travel

Don't leave your luggage unguarded for even a moment. Place an easily identifiable mark on your luggage and have your name and address inside each piece. Learn from this book how to travel light so you don't have to keep track of many pieces of luggage

Your luggage may be legally opened (Patriot Act) and searched both in and out of your presence. Any lock you place on your luggage may be broken. Purchase a safety strap that can be opened and reclosed. Don't wrap packages before travel. You will be asked to unwrap them by security.

33

NOTE: *Magellan's Travel Supply catalog has locked safety straps for luggage and many other safety and convenience items for travelers. Call: 800-962-4943, fax: 800-962-4940, or log on to www.Magellans.com to order a catalog.*

Allow the person in front of you at airport metal detectors to remove their items from the carrier belt before you place your luggage on it. You want to be able to follow right through to pick up your things.

Never carry packages on board for strangers. If anyone approaches you and asks you to carry *anything* on board, refuse and notify security. Be sure no one can get close enough to your purse or carry-on to slip in an item without your knowledge.

If you see an unattended package or suitcase, notify security immediately.

Never joke about having a bomb or firearm in your possession. Security personnel are trained to react when they hear these words. Penalties are severe. They can include fines and/or time in prison.

Be aware of items forbidden on a plane so you don't try to take them with you.

Get in and out of airports as quickly as possible. Unfortunately, crooks like to hang out at airports and take advantage of unwary travelers. Be alert to what is going on around you and where your belongings are at all times.

Avoid purchasing expensive, conspicuous luggage. Dark or neutral colored luggage without designer labels is best. Place a distinctive sticker with meaning for you on the outside of your bag.

Don't wear clothing, shoes, or carry a purse with lots of metal. Examples: metal buttons, belt buckles, shoe buckles or buttons as trim. The presence of the metal will delay your pass though security gates.

Check at the TSA site the list of items not allowed

Flying safely

Airline tickets are almost all e-tickets. You won't be issued a paper ticket. You will receive a printed itinerary with dates, time, flight numbers, and seating. Check it carefully to be sure everything is correct including name, flight dates, times, and confirmations.

Be prepared to have your luggage searched and your person scanned. You must present a photo ID when you fly. Be sure your name on the ID and your name on the tickets matches exactly.

Reconfirm your reservations before each trip because airline schedules sometimes change. On international flights, most airlines require that you reconfirm your departure and return reservations at least 72 hours before each flight. If you don't, your reservations may be canceled.

You must meet the airline's deadline for buying your ticket. Discount tickets must usually be purchased within a certain period after the reservations have been made.

Check in early! The airlines have deadlines for check-in and if you fail to meet them, you may lose your advance seat assignment. Even if you have advance boarding passes for domestic flights, you must check in 30 minutes before the flight is scheduled to leave. On international flights—partly owing to required security procedures —the check-in may be much earlier. Ask your travel agent to obtain the information about check-in times and procedures for you.

TIP: *The best way to avoid being bumped off a flight is to check in early.*

Place tags with your name and address on each bag. Buy luggage tags with a covering flap so observers can't see it easily. Burglars have been known to frequent airports and get addresses of people who obviously won't be home.

Also, stick a label to the inside of the bags with your name, address, phone number and the name and phone number of your contact person who has your itinerary and can always reach you.

Remove all the destination tags from previous trips so busy baggage handlers are not confused.

Lost or damaged luggage

The airline will usually pay for repairs if your suitcase arrives smashed or torn. When your bag is visibly damaged or opened, check for losses. Report problems to the airline *before leaving the airport.* Insist on filling out a report.

Don't panic if your suitcase doesn't show up on the conveyor belt. The airlines have sophisticated tracking methods and find misplaced bags 98 percent of the time. They may even pay for your inconvenience. Report your missing bag before you leave the airport, file a written report (keep a copy) and get the full name of the person to whom you made the report.

If luggage is truly lost, you will have to submit a claim. Don't delay doing the required process. Keep all travel documents and receipts for money you had to spend because of the mishandling. Get the names of every airline employee with whom you deal. Call or write the airline's consumer office when you get home.

Each airline and even different flights on the same airline may have different size and weight requirements for baggage. Check with the airlines you will be using or ask your travel agent to do it for you.

Smoking
As of June, 2000, smoking is prohibited on all domestic and foreign airlines that take off or land in the U.S.

Other plane travel tips
▸ Planes sometimes make sudden stops when taxiing so resist the urge to jump up before the plane comes to a complete stop. Stay in your seat with the seat belt fastened until the "fasten seat belt" sign goes off.

▸ Be careful about what you put in overhead bins. Their doors may pop open during an accident or even a hard landing, spilling the contents. Passengers have been injured by items falling from an overhead bin when it was opened. Place heavy items under the seat and save the overhead bins for softer items.

▸ Before takeoff, there will be a briefing about safety procedures. The flight attendants will point out emergency exits, seat belts, life vests, and oxygen masks. Listen carefully. Even if you have flown many times, the information is important.

▸ Look for the closest exit from the plane and count the number of rows between you and it. Then plan an alternate route should that one be blocked in an emergency situation.

▸ When your plane has reached cruising altitude and the pilot turns off the "fasten seat belt" sign, keep your seatbelt in place unless you need to leave your seat. In case of rough air, you will be safer.

Hazardous items

Never take any of the following hazardous materials on a plane. They are illegal as well as extremely dangerous.

AEROSOLS: Polishes, hair spray, deodorants, etc.

CORROSIVES: Acids, cleaners, wet cell batteries

FLAMMABLES: Paints, thinners, lighter fluid, liquid reservoir lighters, cleaners, adhesives, camp stoves or portable gas equipment with fluid

EXPLOSIVES: Fireworks, flares, signal devices, loaded firearms, gunpowder, etc. (Check with the airlines regarding the very strict regulations about transporting guns on a commercial airliner.)

RADIOACTIVE SUBSTANCES: Betascopes, radio pharmaceuticals, uninstalled pacemakers

COMPRESSED GASES: Tear gas or protective type sprays, oxygen cylinders, divers' tanks (unless they are empty)

INFECTIOUS SUBSTANCES

POISONS: Rat poison, etc.

MATCHES: May only be carried on your person.

SHARPS: Pointed metal scissors, carpet knives, box cutters, ice picks, straight razors, and any device with a folding or retractable blade.

A violation of the hazardous materials restrictions can result in a civil penalty of up to $25,000 for each violation or a criminal penalty of up to $500,000 and/or up to five years in prison. Check with the airline if you even *suspect* you will want to carry an item that could fit into one of the above categories.

Air accidents

If you are ever in an air accident, it is vital to:

▸ **Stay calm!** Panic is your worst enemy.

▸ When it is obvious the plane is going down, **fasten your seat belt tightly**, bend over in your seat and firmly hold a pillow on your face and head.

▸ Take all **sharp objects** out of your pockets and remove glasses and dentures.

▸ Put on a personal **smoke hood** *(available at Magellan's Travel Supply)* or wet a handkerchief or other cloth to hold over your mouth and nose if the cabin fills with smoke.

▸ If you survive the crash, the most important thing you can do to save your life is **get out of there** as fast as you can. As soon as the plane comes to a stop, undo your seat belt, get up quickly and move to the exit

▸ **Don't take anything with you.** You may have to climb over seats or debris and you'll need both hands to get yourself and family members to an exit You'll know you are at an exit when the floor lights show white instead of red.

▸ **Look outside the window** before you try to open any emergency exit. If you see a fire outside the door, don't open it. The flames may spread throughout the cabin. Use your alternate route.

▸ **Smoke rises**, so keep your head down as you move to an exit. Don't get down on the floor to crawl, though. You may be trampled. Follow the track of emergency lights embedded in the floor. They lead to an exit. If you have a cloth, put it over your nose and mouth.

▸ When you are outside the plane, **move away** from it as far as you can. Only when you are safely away, should you pause and assess what you can do to help others.

Attempted highjacking
The best advice used to be to keep quiet since usually the highjackers wanted the plane for some purpose of their own and usually did not harm passengers. However, with terrorists using planes as missiles, the newest advice is for the passengers as a group to throw everything they can at the highjackers, (books, shoes, sodas or whatever) to disarm them and take control of the plane. If the highjackers have guns, this may result in injury or death to some passengers.

Rental cars
When you rent a car, familiarize yourself with all the buttons and dials before you drive away from the rental lot.
▸ Practice turning on and off the ignition.
▸ Check the brakes.
▸ Practice turning on the windshield wipers and lights—including hazard lights.
▸ Know how to open the hood and trunk.
▸ Find out who to call in case of an emergency.
▸ Be sure you have an inflated spare tire and a jack.
▸ Try the locks to be sure they work.
Don't accept a car clearly marked on the license plate or other parts of the vehicle as a rental and don't rent a car without a closed, locked trunk.
Rent a nonsmoking car. They are usually the newest cars in the fleet.

Avoid renting a luxury car. It is flashy and draws the attention of thieves. Plus, gas is very expensive.

Rent a cellular phone when possible. Make a list of numbers you may need.

Keep a disposable camera in your purse or the glove compartment of the car. In case you are in an accident, take pictures.

Keep your clothes, local maps, packages, and luggage out of sight in the car. These items lying about in open view will identify you as a tourist.

Be careful where you park. Pick well-lighted places with people nearby. Look around you before you get in or out of the car. As you approach the car, have your key in your hand, ready to use.

When you are driving, if someone deliberately bumps your car, *don't stop*! Drive on to the nearest well-lighted place with lots of people around. If you see a police officer or police station, pull in there.

Carry a flashlight with you always. If you can, carry an emergency banner (NEED HELP, CALL POLICE) to place in the window when you have an emergency.

Dress and behave conservatively. Avoid showy dress, valuable jewelry, furs, very expensive luggage, or conspicuous behavior that will draw attention to you as a potentially wealthy or important foreigner. Let the golden rule dictate your behavior—be polite and low-key.

Fire safety

When you check in to your hotel, ask how their fire alarm system works. If you don't understand the explanation, ask for a demonstration. Be sure children traveling with you understand the system, too.

Always keep your room key in your handbag beside your bed in the same spot. You can grab it up quickly in case of fire or other emergency.

Memorize the location of fire exits and draw a mental map of the corridors. Sometimes, hotels post a helpful map on the room door. Count the doors to the exit so in case smoke from a fire obscures your vision, you can get to the exit safely. Have a fire drill with your fellow travelers. Rehearse drills two or more times with children.

Check nearby fire exits to be sure the doors are unlocked and unobstructed. Check to see if they close automatically. Complain to the management if you have any doubts.

Select a prearranged meeting place for everyone in your party. In case of an emergency, you can quickly account for everyone. Have "dog tags" made for your children. Have them wear the tags under their clothing at all times. As well as names and addresses, include on the tags.a contact and phone number of someone back home.

In case of fire

► Don't panic! Take a deep breath and stay in control so you can take steps to save your life and the lives of others.

► Report the fire to the fire department first, then to the hotel desk. Give them your room number. Follow the instructions given over an audio system or by hotel staff.

► Touch your room door before opening it. If it's hot, keep it closed.

► Stay in your room if the corridor is filled with smoke. Close the door and stuff towels in the cracks.

► Go the nearest fire exit if the corridor is clear. Close your room door as you leave to keep out smoke. Take your room key so you can get back in when the danger is over or when you can't proceed to an exit.

► Open or break the window if smoke enters your room. Make a wet bed sheet into a tent over your head so you can breathe easier.
► Crouch or crawl if you have to pass through smoke to a clear area. Cover yourself with a wet blanket for protection from heat.
► Have your children go in front of you (if it is safe) so you have them in your sight always.
► Never panic or give up; help may be just minutes away.

When disaster strikes abroad
Most persons travel safely and have wonderful experiences. Individuals can usually handle minor crises with foresight and common sense. However, it always pays to be informed and prepared so that if you are caught up in one of the rare instances when a disaster occurs, you will know what to do. Assess your situation and surroundings wherever you are. Try to maintain a healthy balance in the zone between complacency and paranoia.

The U.S. State Department recommends that you inform the U.S. embassy or consulate when you arrive in a foreign country. It is important to know the address and phone number of the embassy and what they do for U.S. citizens abroad.

The following table gives an overview of the state department's set up for services to citizens overseas.

United States Department of State
⇓
Bureau of Consular Affairs
⇓
Overseas Citizen Services

⇓	⇓	⇓
American Citizens Services and Crises Mgmt	Office of Children's Services	Office of Policy Review & Interagency Liaison

Overseas Citizens Services in the State Department's Bureau of Consular Affairs is responsible for the welfare and whereabouts of U.S. citizens traveling and residing abroad. It has three offices:

1. **American Citizens Services and Crisis Management** assists in all matters involving protective services for Americans abroad, including arrests, death cases, financial or medical emergencies, and welfare and whereabouts inquiries. The office also issues Travel Warnings and Consular Information Sheets and provides guidance in many other areas.

NOTE: Travel warnings are issued when the State Department advises citizens to defer travel to a country because of dangerous conditions or because the U.S. has no diplomatic relations with the country.

Consular Information Sheets contain information on entry requirements, crime and security conditions, areas of instability and other details about travel in a particular country. See more details in the Resource Section of this book.

2. **The Office of Children's Issues** formulates, develops and coordinates policies and programs on international parental child abduction and international adoptions.
3. **The Office of Policy Review and Interagency Liaison** provides guidance on laws, documentation of Americans living abroad. It offers advice about treaties and agreements and legislative matters.

NOTE: *Detailed information about the State Department's services can be found on the Internet at http://travel.state.gov. You can print information, warnings, booklets, and access other government agencies such as the Center for Disease Control.*

Travel Safety List

☐ Identifying mark on luggage

☐ Name and address on the inside and outside luggage

☐ Dog tags and labels

☐ Safety strap on suitcase

☐ Car insurance

☐ Company _____

☐ Policy No. _____

☐ Agent _____

☐ Phone _____

☐ Fax _____

☐ Lights okay

☐ Turn on windshield wiper

☐ Test brakes

☐ Test locks

☐ Emergency phone number

☐ Spare tire and jack

☐ Cellular phone

☐ Address book

☐ Maps and guidebooks

- ☐ Translation book or electronic device
- ☐ Flashlight
- ☐ Banner (NEED HELP–CALL POLICE)
- ☐ First aid kit
- ☐ Hotel alarm system
- ☐ Fire exits
- ☐ Mental map of corridors
- ☐ Emergency phone number for fire department

_____

- ☐ Emergency phone number for medical help

_____

- ☐ Prearrange a meeting place
- ☐ Fire drill with children
- ☐ Overseas Citizen's Services 24 hour hotline number.

_____

- ☐ Local U.S. embassy or consulate phone number.

_____

Chapter Five

PERSONAL SAFETY

Personal Safety measures will depend on where and with whom you are traveling. Independent travel in an undeveloped country will require far more precautions than travel with a guided tour in a developed country. Many precautions are common sense anywhere.

Positive attitude

Attitude has a lot to do with personal safety. Be aware of your surroundings. If something doesn't seem right, trust your intuition and get out of there! If you are accosted, don't be belligerent but don't grovel either. Maintain a calm assertive manner. Give up belongings to an armed person. Don't die for them; your life is more valuable than any possession.

Your body language can invite or deter a potential attacker. Pace, posture and tone of voice are powerful signs of vulnerability or strength. Walk with your head up and eyes peeled. Let your body language be a warning that you are alert and ready to take action. If someone is harassing you, say firmly and assertively, "Leave me alone."

Avoid alcohol or other substances that will decrease your response time and attentiveness when you are in a new or strange place.

Alertness as a safety measure

Learn the layout of the city or part of the country you are visiting. Notice landmarks so you don't get lost. When walking about, have a map but don't wave it about or be conspicuous when using it. Before you leave your hotel, ask the person at the front desk if any areas of the city are best to avoid or if you should take any precautions while walking.

Be careful when walking alone in a strange city. If you are elderly, female, or it's after dark, you are especially vulnerable. Many places have guided walking tours. Not only are they safer, but you will meet people and learn more about the place you are visiting. (Find out about guided walking tours from the tourist bureaus of the various countries.)

Before you leave home, keep track of what is reported in the media about any developments that may jeopardize your safety in the area you plan to visit. The U.S. State Department's Overseas Citizens Services gives travel advisory information twenty-four hours a day. Call 202-647-5225 or or visit their website at *http://travel.state.gov.*

Know how to use a local pay phone and learn the emergency call number for the country. Check street names and landmarks so you can identify your location if necessary.

Carry a credit card, not cash. Keep your money and other valuables in the hotel or ship's safe. Hiding your valuables in your room makes it easy for burglars. They make it their business to know all the hiding places. Take out of the safe only the amount of money you need each day or better yet, use your credit card to get the money you need at an ATM machine.

Take only one or two credit cards when you travel. Visa, MasterCard, and American Express are best. You should be able to use one card in an ATM. Make a copy of your cards. Know the number to call if a card is lost or stolen. If you have a travel companion, carry-one card and have your companion carry the other.

Know your credit card limit and don't exceed it. Americans have been arrested in some countries for innocently going over their limit.

Frequent ATMs during the day when people are around. Be careful when you use your card so that persons standing nearby cannot see your PIN as you enter it into the machine.

To guard against thieves on motorcycles, walk on the inside of sidewalks. Your bag should have a closed top and sturdy shoulder straps. The straps should be short enough so the bag is under your arm, close to your body, when carried. Carry it on the shoulder away from the curb.

WARNING: *Don't put the strap of a purse or bag across your chest or around your neck. You could be injured if a determined thief pulls on them.*

Spread your valuables around your person rather than keeping them all in your purse or bag. Purchase or make carriers you can tuck into your belt or around your neck inside your clothing. Many styles and materials are available at travel supply stores. Check the list of stores in the Resource Section of this book.

TIP: *Wrapping rubber bands around your wallet makes it more difficult for a pickpocket to remove it from your pocket without your knowledge.*

Report thefts to the police or other appropriate authorities immediately. Keep a copy of the police report for insurance claims.

Report the loss of travelers' checks to the nearest office of the issuing agent.

Report the loss of airline tickets to the airline or your travel agent.

Report the loss of your passport to the nearest U.S. embassy or consulate. *Replacement can be difficult. See the suggestions in the passport section of this book.*

Cultural considerations

When you are in a foreign country, you should be aware of cultural customs to avoid embarrassment or harassment. Remember, you can do many things in the U.S. and other democracies that you can't do elsewhere.

Examples:

▸ In Muslim countries, immodestly dressed women may be arrested, spit upon, or attacked.

▸ In India, leather shoes and accessories may be offensive to Hindus who revere cows.

▸ In Rome, sightseers who strip down to shorts and bikinis are liable to be ordered to cover up. Sunbathing or bathing in the city's fountains brings a stiff fine. Avoid problems by dressing modestly. Save beach attire for the beach.

▸ Joining a political demonstration, taking photographs without permission, engaging in formal or informal missionary work, drinking alcohol, swimming naked or merely talking to the wrong people are enough to attract the attention of police in several countries. In some places, police brutality is the norm and civil rights are unknown or irrelevant.

Learn about a country's customs, laws and religious observances before you travel. Travel agents have information, the State Department has booklets, and many travel guides and books are available.

The U.S. State Department is very concerned about the number of American citizens involved in narcotics cases. In many countries, arrests can mean lengthy confinement, hard labor, heavy fines, and even death.

The U.S. Embassy cannot get a prisoner released or represent a defendant at a trial. Just as foreigners are subject to U.S. laws when in the U.S., Americans are subject to the law of the land where they travel.

Trusting tourists can be drawn into crime when they carry a package for someone. Never carry something across borders or on a plane for someone. You will pay the penalty, not them.

Some countries have become jittery about the use of video recorders by tourists. Don't try to film disturbances or the insides of sacred shrines. Ask someone in authority if filming is okay, especially if you have any doubts.

Try to arrive at your destination during daylight hours when people are around and it's easier to get oriented. At night, identifying landmarks is difficult so safety is more of an issue.

Hotel safety

Always keep your hotel room locked. If someone you don't know comes to the door, ask their business before you open the door. Call the hotel management to investigate (before you open the door) if you have any doubts. Carry a door stop as an extra precaution. Magellan's catalog sells them *(see Resource Section)*.

▸ When you first arrive in your room, check to see that the phone is working. Hotels sometimes shut off the phones in uninhabited rooms to prevent unauthorized calls.

▸ Don't leave hotel or car keys lying around. Keep them out of sight on your person. Many European countries have you turn in your key when you are out of your room. Be sure hotel desk staff know who can and cannot claim the key. Remind the person on duty at the desk every time you leave the key.

- Check elevators before you enter, especially if you are alone. Avoid entering an elevator when you are alone and a stranger is in it.
- Leave the lights and a radio or television on when you are out of your room so it seems occupied.
- Reserve a room opening onto an inside corridor. Outside rooms are more accessible to thieves.
- Don't leave a "Please clean this room" sign on your door. It is a signal to crooks that you are out.
- Meet new acquaintances in the lobby. Don't invite strangers to your room.
- When you are shopping, don't load yourself down with packages. Have your purchases delivered to your hotel.
- Don't wear high heels and tight skirts when walking about or shopping. They limit your mobility.

Personal Safety List

- ☐ Check travel advisories
- ☐ Credit cards _____
- ☐ Credit card limit _____
- ☐ Local police number _____
- ☐ Valuables carrier
- ☐ Door stop
- ☐ Street Maps
- ☐ Customs to be aware of _____

_____

_____

_____

_____

Chapter Six

HEALTH CARE

Having an accident or illness at home is bad but when you are far from home and don't know the local medical system or doctors, it can be frightening and difficult to resolve. Even if you are in good health, you need to be aware of hazards you may encounter while traveling in foreign places. Learn what to do and where to get help before you travel. It will give you peace of mind.

Of course, if you do have a health problem, planning is essential if you are to enjoy your travel.

See your doctor

See your doctor for a physical examination before you travel. Discuss your plans with him or her. Give the doctor information about the climate and the amount and type of exercise you will be doing. Ask for advice about the health aids and medication you need to take with you. Decide together if you will be able to complete the planned travel without undue risk.

Ask your doctor to write three prescriptions for each of your medications. Have two of each filled. Carry-one set of the medication in your carry-on bag. Pack the second set of medications in your suitcase. Leave the third copy of your prescriptions at home with a person you can call if necessary. Now you have two backups so you can get refills easily if your medications are lost or stolen.

Ask your doctor to type or print legibly all the prescriptions and other medical information he gives you. Keep your doctor's name, address and phone number with your emergency information.

You *must* have a letter from your doctor, dated and signed, stating why you need needles, syringes, narcotics or hypnotics if you have a medical condition requiring you to carry them. The letter must be on the doctor's letterhead and all items listed. Medications should be listed by generic as well as trade names. Insist the letter be typed. It must be completely legible. Don't leave home without it! The penalties in many countries for unauthorized or illegal possession and transport of these items are severe and may even include death!

NOTE: Send for a government information booklet on the subject. See the Resource Section of this book.

All your prescription and over-the-counter medication must be carried in their original packaging. Don't remove any medications from their packages until you are ready to swallow them. Keep all medications and medical devices in their original packaging until *after* you clear customs on your return home.

Think twice about purchasing medications out of the country. The strength and dosage may be different from what you are accustomed to using.

Never take medications purchased out of the country back home with you. The medications may be controlled substances in your country and you could be arrested for smuggling. At the least, the medication will be confiscated and a report made— time-consuming when you are tired and want to get home.

The Center for Disease Control in Atlanta, Georgia has up-to-date information about vaccination recommendations, travel with children, reference material, outbreaks, special needs travelers, diseases, safe food and water, and health information on cruise ships. They also have health information on specific travel destination and travelers' health warnings. The toll-free phone number is 877-FYI-TRIP. The toll-free fax number for requesting information is 888-232-3299 or see their website at *www.cdc.gov*

Health issues

▸ **Allergies.** Wear a medic alert bracelet or necklace. Inform your travel companions and the tour guide (if on a tour) about your allergies and what to do if you need help. Carry the medications you need in a separate reclosable plastic bag with written instructions for their use in case you can't speak for yourself. Check *www.aafa.org*, the website for the Asthma and Allergy Foundation of America for specific information about your allergy.

▸ **Altitude sickness.** You may experience distressing symptoms in altitudes over 3000 feet. Some of the symptoms may include dizziness, loss of appetite, nausea, mental confusion, headache, and shortness of breath. Your body will usually adjust to the new altitude in a few days if you have no complicating illness. Eat lightly, drink lots of fluid, and take short naps during the day while your body is adjusting. Don't drink alcohol.

NOTE: Persons with asthma, emphysema, heart disease and chronic lung disease will suffer more. They may not tolerate the decreased amount of oxygen in the air and will have to return to a lower altitude.

▸ **Constipation.** The changes in your normal schedule, including different foods, jet lag, and just being away from your normal routine can lead to constipation. The following preventive measures will help.

1. Eat high fiber foods and drink eight to ten glasses of cool water each day
2. Exercise daily
3. Take a bulk producing preparation such as Metamucil™.
4. Take Colace™ (a stool softener) before bedtime if the above measures aren't effective.
5. Don't take laxatives. They prolong irregularity and they are unpredictable. Imagine the laxative saying, *"NOW!"* when no toilet is available.

NOTE: *Never take any kind of stool softener, laxative, suppository, or enema if you have acute abdominal pain, nausea, and/or fever. See a doctor immediately.*

▸ **Diabetes.** Insulin dependent diabetics should take all their supplies with them including insulin, syringes, and testing equipment. Insulin is available in most countries but the strength and brand may be different from what you use. You can order a specially designed travel case, complete with cold pack, from Medicool Inc., 23520 Telo Ave. # 6, Torrance CA 90505. Call 800-433-2469 to order a catalog or visit their website at www.medicool.com.
In addition:

1. Always carry water (enough for a pint an hour) and a high carbohydrate snack.
2. Wear a medic alert bracelet or necklace. Order from Medic-Alert, 2323 Colorado Ave., Turlock CA 95382. Call 800-432-5378 to request a catalog or visit their website at *www.medicalert.org*

3.   Join IAMAT (International Association of Medical Assistance to Travelers). *(see Resource Section).*

4.   Take precautions to protect your feet from blisters and wounds.

5.   Be sure your travel companions know how to help you if you need it.

NOTE: Be sure you have a letter from your doctor stating you are diabetic and require injections.

▸ **Diarrhea.** You may have heard jokes about travelers' diarrhea but it is no laughing matter. Not only can it ruin your travel, it can permanently effect your health and cause death.

Common sense precautions include the following:

1.   Wash your hands with soap before meals, before putting your hands and fingers in your mouth, after using the toilet and after handling things in stores or markets. In third world countries, take a package of antiseptic wipes.

2.   Don't drink the local water unless you are positive it is safe.

3.   Be sure bottled water is sealed at the factory before you buy it.

4.   In suspect areas, don't eat fruit and vegetables that you cannot peel.

Even with precautions, you may get diarrhea. Take Kaopectate™, Pepto-Bismol™, or Immodium™ with you in your health kit. Use only as directed. If you have a fever, do not take Immodium™ without first consulting a doctor.

Each day you have diarrhea, do the following:

1. Drink eight to ten glasses of water with a pinch of baking soda and a pinch of salt in each glassful.
2. Drink large quantities of salty broth. You need the salt and soda along with the fluids to keep your system in balance.
3. Avoid spicy foods, fats, and milk products.
4. Eat frequent, small amounts of bland food such as hot, freshly cooked plain rice or barley.

CAUTION: After using all the suggestions above, if you continue to have diarrhea for more than three days, notice blood in your stool, feel weak or disoriented, see a doctor immediately.

▸ **Foot care.** You can be sure you will be on your feet many hours a day when you travel. Take steps to be sure your feet in good condition before you go.
1. See a podiatrist to resolve any problems.
2. Give yourself regular foot care. This includes massage with lotion and care of nails.
3. Take well-fitted, well broken in shoes with you.
4. Wear socks or stockings, but avoid the type with elastic at the top.
5. Prop your feet up higher than your heart whenever you have the chance.
6. Begin a walking program several weeks before you travel. Walk 15 minutes a day at a moderate pace. Increase your time by 5 minutes every few days as you can tolerate it. Walk every day and increase time until you can walk two miles in 30 minutes. When you begin the walking program, begin lifting weights also. Consult a gym or a physical therapist or read about walking programs in Prevention and other popular magazines.

▸ **Heart problems**. The most frequent serious health emergency to befall travelers is heart problems.

A physical exam is important for anyone planning to travel but if you have heart problems, consulting with your doctor is vital. Discuss a safe activity level, medication, and other issues relevant to your health status.

Regular aerobic exercise (such as brisk walking) for at least 30 minutes, three to four times a week, contributes immeasurably to a healthy heart and lungs. Starting your exercise regimen at least three months before you travel is optimal, but if you have less time than that, start now. It could make a big difference. Check with your doctor for your exercise limits.

Maintain a relaxed mental attitude. Refuse to allow the inevitable little things that go wrong to upset you.

Should you have chest pain that does not go away with rest, it is imperative to call for medical help immediately! Chew up an aspirin and rest in a semi-sitting position until help arrives.

▸ **Heat Exhaustion.** This medical emergency occurs when a person not used to hot weather is exposed to it for too long and, at the same time, is not drinking enough water.

Symptoms include excess sweating, cool and clammy skin, and an increased pulse rate. The person may also experience nausea, dizziness, weakness, headaches, and muscle cramps.

Heat exhaustion can be prevented with a few common sense precautions:

1. Drink plenty of water. (Now, where have you read that before!) If you will be away from a safe water source, carry enough so you can drink four to eight ounces an hour. Add a

pinch of salt and baking soda to each quart or take along a salty snack.

2. Don't overexert yourself in the heat. Stop to rest in the shade frequently.

3. Wear a ventilated, brimmed hat. An all-around wide brim offers the best sun shielding.

4. Seek out shade in which to walk or rest.

If you experience any of the symptoms of heat exhaustion, move to a shady spot or out of the heat completely as soon as possible. Rest and drink lots of mildly salty fluids.

▸ **Heat stroke.** Heat stroke occurs with prolonged exposure or exertion in hot conditions and not drinking enough water. The heat regulator in the brain shuts down and the body temperature rapidly rises to 104° F. or higher. The person is flushed, has hot, dry skin and may lose consciousness.

Heat stroke is a life-threatening emergency. Get medical help without delay. Call an ambulance if you can.

Away from immediate medical facilities, first aid can save a life. Take the following steps.

1. Move the person to the coolest available place. Make shade with whatever you can such as, clothes strung on branches, etc.

2. Lay the victim on his or her back with a rolled up towel (or whatever you have) under the neck to tilt the head back to keep the airway open.

3. Wrap the person, front, back, and head in a cloth soaked in water. No cloth? Thoroughly wet their clothing until it is dripping. Wet the whole body and head (important. Wrap a cloth around the head).

4. Sponge the person's face with a wet cloth.

5. Fan the person with a hand held paper, branch, or whatever you have. Turn the person from side to side so the entire body is fanned.
6. Keep the clothes or body covering sopping wet and continue fanning until the person's body temperature drops below 100° F or the pulse rate goes down to about 80 beats per minute.
7. When the person is fully conscious, elevate the head and give small sips of water every five minutes. Add a pinch of salt and soda to each quart of water.
8. Keep the person wet and continue fanning until medical help arrives.

▶ **Immunizations.** Check with your local public health agency, the Center for Disease Control hotline or website, your physician, or a physician specializing in travel health to find out which immunizations you need for your travel.

Carry your yellow, international vaccination card with you when you travel.

▶ **Jet lag.** Rapid travel across multiple time zones is what usually causes jet lag. The most severe cases are apt to affect people traveling from west to east.

You can take steps before you travel and after you arrive at your destination to lessen the effects of jet lag.

1. Before you travel, find out the time difference between your home and where you are going. Gradually adjust your sleep and eating schedule to the new time zone.
2. Sip on an electrolyte sports drink (preferably sugar free) during the flight.
3. On the flight, avoid alcohol. It is dehydrating and can worsen jet lag symptoms.

4.   Avoid sleeping pills. They can cause confusion and transient memory loss.
5.   On a night flight, try to sleep during the hours you will be sleeping at your destination.
6.   When you arrive, rest and relax the first day. Eat and sleep in your current time zone. Exercise daily in fresh air and sunshine to reset your biological clock.

▸ **Motion sickness.** Preventing motion sickness is easier than curing it once it has begun. Try to sit where the least amount of motion occurs, such as in the middle of the ship or over the wings of the airplane. Make sure there is a fresh air flow. Eat and drink in moderation before and during your travel.

A non-medicine solution for prevention of motion sickness is *Sea-Bands*. These stretchy wrist bands help curb nausea and vomiting by exerting acupressure against key points on the wrists. Studies have shown them to be effective, with no known side effects. People of any age can use them. Find them at travel shops, pharmacies and through travel catalogs for about $9 a pair.

Another non-medicine remedy is called the Relief Band. You wear it on your wrist like a watch. It sends gentle electric signals to the underside of the wrist. The band is FDA approved for motion sickness. You can buy them over the counter for $35 to $50. Log onto *www.reliefbands.com.*

Medication can be used to prevent motion sickness. Dramamine™, Marezine™, Phenergan™ and Benadryl™ are all non-prescription drugs you can use. Take the medications about 30 minutes before exposure to motion, then every four to six hours for 24 hours. Don't take the medication for longer than 48 hours. The main side effect of these medications is drowsiness.

▸ **Sex and the traveler.** More than 30 sexually transmitted diseases (STD) have now been identified. Should you choose to have sex with someone you encounter on your travels, you run the risk of contracting any STD your partner got from a previous sexual encounter. In essence (as far as microorganisms are concerned) when you have sex with a person, you are having sex with all the person's previous partners.

When you meet a charming crew member on a ship and get "swept away" by his charisma, stop and think before you hop into bed with him. Chances are you would not be the first person he has had sex with on a cruise. You may take home a souvenir from him that alters your life.

Sex addicts are attracted to jobs that put them in contact with a constant flow of prospective sex partners. They are not interested in you as a person, only as a means of assuaging their addiction. Use your common sense and don't be victimized. A relationship based on mutual respect and affection doesn't happen overnight.

If you decide to take a chance, at least avoid unprotected sex.

▸ **Stress.** Feeling anxious or estranged in a different culture is common in travelers. Some people manage to remain relaxed and easygoing in most situations. For others, even a small problem becomes a catastrophe and a source of stress and worry. Accepting the idea that you cause this way of thinking and thus generate your anxiety may be difficult for you. Nonetheless, it is often true.

Do you often find yourself going over and over a problem? For example, saying "what if..." or reliving the details for hours. Traveling presents many new situations and things may not always go according to your plans. However, in terms of your mental health, you make the experience worse by ruminating over it.

Say to yourself instead, "I don't like having this problem but I will do what I can about it, then drop it. I refuse to allow it to ruin my day." Practice this rational self-talk often. It has amazing power.

Learn simple relaxation techniques. Cassette tapes and CDs are available at most bookstores. Relaxation and regular exercise both contribute to the reduction of stress.

Avoid tranquilizers. They are addictive and have many side effects.

Don't be compulsive about sightseeing, shopping, or any other activity. You are on vacation to have a good time; relax as you choose your preferred pace.

Remember, " *'Twas for your pleasure you came here."*
William Cowper

► **Sun protection.** Always protect yourself from the direct rays of the sun. Use a PABA-free sunscreen of 15 to 45 SPF. Apply at least 30 minutes *before* going out in the sun to every part of your body that will be exposed. (It takes that long for the sun screen to soak into your skin and protect it.) Reapply every four hours or more often if you are very fair and after swimming. Don't forget the tips of your ears, your nose and the tops of your feet. These parts of your body are very vulnerable to sun burn.

Wear a broad-brimmed hat to protect your head, face, and neck. A sport hat with only a front brim does not provide adequate protection for your ears and the back of your neck.

Wear light-colored loose clothing when you are out of the water rather than expose a lot of skin to the sun's rays..

Stay indoors from 11 a.m. to 3 p.m. when the sun is most intense. People in hot countries take a siesta during those hours. You would do well to imitate them.

Use a 15-SPF lip balm and reapply frequently.

Drink lots of water. Sports drinks have some benefit but they usually contain too much sugar. Sugar free fruit juice or vegetable juice is better. Drink it in addition to your water.

Compact, convenient travelers' health items and specially designed clothing for easy-care, and good looks are available from stores specializing in travel items. They can add to your comfort when you travel (*see Resource Section*).

▸ **Teeth.** Before you go on an extended trip, especially to an undeveloped country, have your dental work up to date. Most insurance companies won't pay for more than emergency care when you are out of the country.

Magellan's travel catalog has a dental emergency kit you can buy. Be sure to take your dental floss or any supplies you use regularly. (*see Resource Section*)

The International Association for Medical Assistance to Travelers (IAMAT) is a great service for travelers. They charge no membership fee, though they do request a donation. You get a membership card entitling you to a world directory of participating physicians in 550 countries and territories. All the doctors have been screened and all were trained in an English-speaking country. IAMAT physicians have agreed to a set fee for office or hotel visits. Visits on Sundays, nights and local holidays cost a bit more.

When you join IAMAT, they send you a passport sized record for your medical history and world immunization chart. You may request other informational brochures on subjects such as

▸ Sanitary condition of water, milk and food in foreign cities.

▸ Infectious diseases such as malaria.

IAMAT membership is not an insurance policy. It is a valuable supplement to travel insurance. Write IAMAT, 417 Center Street, Lewiston, NY 14092, call 716-754-4883 or see their website at *http://www.iamat.org* for more information and an application.

Medic-Alert

Wear a medic-alert bracelet or necklace if you have chronic or life-threatening diseases or allergies. Medical alert bracelets, necklaces and a medical card will give valuable information so travelers can obtain help when they are unable to speak for themselves. Call 800-432-5378, write to Medic-Alert, 2323 Colorado Ave, Turlock, CA 95382 or log on to their website at *www.medicalert.org.*

Medical and First Aid List

☐ Physical exam completed

☐ Three prescriptions for each medicine.

☐ Medication _____

☐ Medication _____

☐ Medication . _____

☐ Medication _____

☐ Medication _____

☐ Doctor _____

Address _____

_____

Phone _____

Fax _____

☐ Letter from doctor explaining need for: needles, syringes, narcotics

☐ Center for Disease Control Information.

☐ Medic-Alert bracelet or necklace obtained.

☐ Dental exam complete

Diabetic supplies

- ☐ Kit from Medicool, Inc.
- ☐ Insulin
- ☐ Test kit
- ☐ Needles/syringes
- ☐ Oral medication

☐ Joined IAMAT

☐ Sunscreen

☐ Sunglasses

☐ Broad-brimmed hat

☐ Lip balm

☐ Alcohol wipes

☐ Betadine wipes

☐ Tinactin™ or Micatin™ for athlete's foot and other fungal infections.

☐ Baking soda. ½ cup in small reclosable plastic bag.

☐ Bandaids—large and small

☐ Birth control

☐ Body powder

☐ Benadryl™ or Chlortrimeton™ for colds, or allergies

- ☐ Metamucil™ or Colace™ for constipation.
- ☐ Cotton swabs for multiple uses.
- ☐ Immodium™, kaopectate or Pepto-Bismol™ for diarrhea
- ☐ Artificial tears for eye care. A box of one dose vials with no preservative.
- ☐ Tucks™, Preparation H™ for hemorrhoids.
- ☐ Tums™, Pepto-Bismol™ for indigestion
- ☐ Johnson's Off ™ for insect control
- ☐ Malaria prophylaxis. (Prescription)
- ☐ Triple antibiotic cream or Neosporin™ for minor cuts, scratches, and blisters.
- ☐ Dramamine™, Phenergan™, or Marezine™ for motion sickness.
- ☐ Sea-Bands to prevent motion sickness.
- ☐ Aspirin, Tylenol, ibuprofen for pain and fever.
- ☐ Hydrocortisone ointment for rashes, insect bites.
- ☐ Salt in individual packets or in a small bag
- ☐ Sanitary napkins
- ☐ Tampons

- ☐ Sunscreen 15-SPF or higher.
- ☐ Solarcaine™ spray for sunburn
- ☐ Tweezers
- ☐ Small scissors
- ☐ Lotion
- ☐ Water bottle—light weight but insulated to keep water cool is best
- ☐ Thermometer
- ☐ Children's fever and pain reliever
- ☐ Sharp needle in a protective holder.
- ☐ Small bag or case to carry first aid supplies.
- ☐ First aid book (The Red Cross sells a good one.)

Chapter Seven

TRAVEL WITH CHILDREN

Traveling with your children can be a rewarding experience for the entire family or it can be the trip from hell. Much of the outcome depends on you and how you prepare your children for travel. The following tips may help.

▸ Teach your children boundaries. Make sure they will comply when you say "No" or "Stop." In a risky situation, you don't want them to be hurt because they haven't learned to listen to you. Teach children to abstain from making remarks out loud about how people look and dress. Have them direct their remarks or questions to you later.

▸ Several times before your trip, take your children out to eat at a sit down restaurant so they know how to behave in this setting. Show them how to order, how to speak to a server and ask for what they want. Teach them good table manners. Expect them to stay in their seats during the meal. Be reasonable, however. Don't expect young children to sit through a lengthy meal of several courses without becoming restless.

Keep children safe

▸ Be sure your children know the first and last names of everyone with whom they will be traveling. Make a game of having them repeat the names of their travel companions several times. They should know their parents' full names, not just Mom and Dad. Teach them their full name and the name of the town where you live.

▸ Teach your children the name of the hotel where you are staying, the phone number, and the room number. Show them how to call the front desk and what number to call in an emergency. Write the numbers in block print and tape near the phone.

▸ Don't let children carry a hotel room key. They can be victimized easily.

▸ Keep your children in sight at all times in airports, bus stations, and train stations. Teach your child a "family code word." Tell them never to go with a person who doesn't know the code word. Teach them to scream and run away if they feel threatened.

▸ Dress your child in bright, easy-to-spot colors. When you have more than one child, dress them in the same colors so you can more easily remember the color.

▸ Don't put children's first names on their clothes or backpacks. A person looking for a child to snatch may disarm them when calling them by name.

▸ Establish a family buddy system so no child goes anywhere alone—including a public bathroom.

▸ Don't allow your children to go to video arcades or darkened movie theaters alone.

▸ Purchase metal "dog tags" imprinted with information that won't change for each child. Include their name, age, parents' names, address. Add the name and phone number of a close relative or friend back home who can serve as a go-between if you become separated from your child.

▸ Make tags for each of your destinations. Cardboard hang tags with strings on them work well and are easy to move when the child changes clothes. Each day, tie the appropriate hang tag on the chain of the child's "dog tags."

Print their name, your name, your local address, and phone number on the tag. If you know the addresses and phone numbers on your itinerary, you can make the tags at home before you leave.

▸ If your children are babies or toddlers, take along a few outlet covers. Use large rubber bands to tie cabinet handles together.

▸ Make sure your child cannot get into any liquor in the minibar.

▸ Check the temperature of the hot water heater where you are staying. It should be no more than 120° or set on low or warm.

▸ One parent must keep an eye on children *every single second* they are near a pool. One of my small nieces nearly drowned while her mother's attention was on something else for only a few minutes

▸   Always have a recent photo of your child with you. Notice carefully what your child is wearing before they leave you.

▸ Register with the U.S. embassy or consulate at each destination.

Health

▸ Take your children for a physical exam before the trip. Ask the doctor for any precautions you should take with your child. Check with the Center for Disease Control for travel advisories.

▸ Take medication you may need for fever and pain. Include a thermometer with your first aid items.

▸ When you arrive at your destination, check the location of the nearest emergency or urgent care facility and IAMAT doctor.

▸ Don't sedate your children before air travel. Indiscriminately medicating children is dangerous.
▸ Try to schedule a night flight so your child can sleep normal hours.
▸ Give your baby a bottle or the breast to suck on during plane take offs and landings. Give your older children gum to chew on. These simple measures will equalize the pressure in their ears and prevent pain.
▸ Take along healthy snacks and liquids. The airlines often serve nuts which children can choke on.
▸ Buckle your child into an approved safety seat while traveling in planes or cars. Do not try to save money by having your small child sit on your lap. If there is heavy turbulence or an accident, the child could be torn from your arms or crushed between you and the seat in front of you.
▸ Ask for positive proof that milk, cheese and other dairy products are pasteurized.
▸ Drink only bottled water in areas where water is not safe. This includes ice cubes. Caution children about drinking pool, lake or river water when swimming.
▸ Join IAMAT. *(see Resource Section)*

Luggage and packing

Parents Law: The smaller the child, the more stuff you need to carry.

Clothing for babies and toddlers doesn't take much space in your luggage. However, you will probably have equipment to manage, too. You will need to plan on doing laundry often.

Disposable diapers are available in most European countries. Verify availability in specific countries with your travel agent or on the internet.

Car seats, child carriers, and strollers are cumbersome to carry but miserable to do without. Before you leave, purchase a combination car seat and stroller. Canvas child carriers are compact and easy to use. Baby beds may be rented at some hotels. If you rent an apartment or house, you can request one as part of the furnishings.

Make or buy each child aged three and up a brightly colored backpack. Buy or make the backpacks in the same colors for each of your children. Make sure the size of the pack is appropriate to the size of the child.

In each backpack, pack:
- A change of clothes
- Extra underpants for toddlers
- A sweater
- Snacks such as graham crackers, fruit, raisins, and juice in individual containers

Add any of the following items appropriate for your child.
- Small spoon and fork
- Spill-proof cup
- Picture book
- Favorite can't-sleep-without-it toy or blanket
- A plastic bib with a large front pocket
- Color books, activity books, puzzle books
- Colored pencils (less messy than crayons or markers).
- Camera and film
- Notebook or journal, pen or pencil, and glue stick.
- Book about the places you will be visiting.
- Puzzle or toy

TIP: You can make sturdy, vinyl-lined backpacks for children and adults from patterns available at most fabric stores. Sew an easily recognized patch on each one. Put your child's name and address inside the backpack.

Encourage children to keep a journal of their vacation. They can collect postcards, flowers, leaves, restaurant napkins, and photos to paste in their journals. Each day sit with them while you write in your travel journal and they write in theirs. They will be the stars of "show and tell" in school next year! In later years, they will enjoy the personal records of their trip.

Clothes
Bright, lightweight cotton-blend knits are good travel choices for children. Both boys and girls can wear shorts, long pants, tank tops and tee shirts for sightseeing, eating out, and most other family activities.

Of course, if your plans include formal occasions, you will need appropriate clothes for the children, too.

Lay out the child's clothing for the trip. Place one complete outfit—top, pants, socks and underwear in a large reclosable plastic bag for each day. At least every seven days, plan to do laundry. If you have an apartment with a washer and dryer or are visiting a private home, this is a breeze. If not, you will need to locate a laundromat.

Additional items to pack include:
- A jacket, hooded sweatshirt or cardigan sweater.
- Three extra pairs of pants or shorts and tee shirts.
- Two or three extra underpants
- Shoes and sandals.
- Lightweight rain gear, including shoe covers.
- Pajamas
- Toothbrush, and hairbrush or comb.

- ▸ Soap, soap dish, and shampoo they use at home.
- ▸ Medications (if any)

Babies

As every parent knows, you will need to wash clothes oftener when you have a baby in diapers. Check the safety and availability of baby supplies and pack accordingly. For instance, if water quality is suspect, don't take powdered formula.

Be sure you have a passport for each child. (see passport section in Chapter 1.)

Children's Travel List

*Child's Name*_____

- ☐ Passport
- ☐ Metal identification tags (dog tags) on a neck chain
- ☐ Paper tags with strings
- ☐ Physical exam
- ☐ Thermometer
- ☐ Medication
- ☐ Seven sets of clothes in reclosable plastic bags
- ☐ Pajamas
- ☐ Rain gear
- ☐ Toothbrush
- ☐ Comb or brush
- ☐ Sweater or jacket
- ☐ Shoes and sandals
- ☐ Extra pants
- ☐ Extra tee shirts
- ☐ Dressy clothes
- ☐ Backpacks with contents
- ☐ Extra underpants for toddlers
- ☐ A sweater

- ☐ Snacks such as, graham crackers, fruit, raisins, juice in individual containers
- ☐ Small spoon and fork
- ☐ Spillproof cup
- ☐ Picture book
- ☐ Favorite can't-sleep-without-it toy or blanket
- ☐ A plastic bib with large front pocket
- ☐ Color books, activity books, puzzle books
- ☐ Colored pencils (less messy than crayons or markers)
- ☐ Camera and film
- ☐ Notebook or journal, pen or pencil, and glue stick
- ☐ Book about the places you will be visiting
- ☐ Puzzle or toy
- ☐ Name of hotel
  - ☐ Address of hotel
  - ☐ Phone number of hotel
  - ☐ How to call front desk
- ☐ Outlet covers
- ☐ Large rubber bands
- ☐ Recent photo of each family member
- ☐ Family code word _____

NOTE: *Copy this list for each child*

Chapter Eight

YOUR TRAVEL AGENT

Travel planning is fun and exciting. However, it takes more than anticipation to make a memorable vacation. Whether your travel plans include a guided tour, a cruise, independent travel, or other adventures, your best source of help is a travel agent.

Travel agents have at their fingertips multiple travel resources—hotels, tours, cruises, airlines, trains, and much more. Most importantly, their experience in planning and booking travel all over the world is at your disposal. They know—or can quickly find out—if the quaint hotel you heard about from Billy's aunt is really a bargain or a miserably-run flea trap in a dangerous part of town.

You have a wide spectrum of travel choices. Review the multitude of exciting options before you decide. With the expert advice of your travel agent, you get the best price for the travel plan of your dreams.

Your agent is probably as excited about traveling as you are. They bring that enthusiasm, along with their expertise, to you.

Of course, every travel agent is not alike. If you meet one who is not listening to you, doesn't seem to understand what you want or is not interested, go to another agent or agency.

As with any business, some people may be cold, disinterested, or difficult. It is important that you feel comfortable with your agent so don't put up with a lackadaisical attitude. It's your money!

Travel agency characteristics

‣ Some travel agencies have a client newsletter or a website. When you call, ask for a copy or the website address. Good newsletters and web pages will have news about special offers, travel tips, information about destinations and, profiles of their agents. The profiles give you an idea of the agent's experience and areas of specialization.

‣ Some agencies give workshops, slide shows, videos, or talks in the community. The workshop schedule of talks or other events is listed in their newsletter and, often, in the local newspaper.

‣ Good travel agencies furnish ongoing training for their agents to keep them up-to-date on the travel industry. This training may be in the form of actual travel to destinations so agents have first hand experience.

‣ Some agencies have agents who are specialists in business travel, senior travel, single travel, family travel, or travel planning for disabled persons. Most agencies can help make plans for all of the above, but for special needs or more expertise, look for a specialist.

The travel business has changed in recent years. Most travel agencies now charge a fee for services and tickets reservations. Considering the amount of service and the time involved in many travel plans, the small fee is a bargain.

Working with a travel agent

Call around. When you find an agent with a positive approach and who sounds eager to begin working with you, make an appointment to discuss your plans.

During your first visit, assess whether this person has the expertise and interest in you as a client to give you the travel experience you want. If you conclude this is the person with whom you want to work, this jewel can truly enrich your travel experiences.

What can you expect at your first appointment with a travel agent?

The agent should ask you the following questions.

- When do you plan to travel?
- What is your total budget?
- Where have you decided to go?
- Will you want a guided tour, semi-independent travel, independent travel, a cruise, etc.?

You may then be shown you a dazzling array of full-color brochures about your desired destination. The brochures show you much of what is available and can help make your decision easier.

Take the brochures home and look them over carefully. Read the small print on the back. Look at the wording inside about the features of the trip or hotels. "Near the ocean" may be a mile or more away. "You will see this town, and that town." may mean you see them from the bus window as you drive by. Make notes of your concerns, then ask your agent lots of questions so you know *exactly* what you are getting.

After you have chosen one to three options for your trip, call your agent again. He or she will contact the companies to check availability and prices and ask the questions on your list.

When you make your final choice, the agent makes your reservations and collects your deposit. At this point, he or she should be able to tell you the documents you will need, such as a passport, visas, inoculations, insurance, or international driver's license. (See Chapter One.)

TIP: If you need medical clearance or any special considerations when you travel, be sure to let your agent know before you book your travel—preferably at your first meeting.

After receiving your final papers and tickets, your agent will go over them carefully to be sure they are complete and that you understand them. Check them over with the agent and ask any final questions.

Your agent can help you while you are traveling. If you have problems with a hotel or car rental, for example, you can call your travel agent to intervene. While you are planning your travel, ask your agent about this ancillary assistance. Don't forget to take your agent's phone number with you on your trip.

NOTE: While you can make your own reservations on the Internet, I enjoy the personal contact with a knowledgeable travel agent. I find the range of options they have at their command saves me time, money, and hassles..

Additional services
▸ Books and videos about your destination
▸ Referral to travel supply companies
▸ Airport van reservations or referrals
▸ Car rental
▸ RailEurope and Britrail passes
▸ Insurance

Your obligations
You have some obligations when working with a travel agent. It is counterproductive to go to several agents and have them all work out itineraries for you. In the first place, all travel connections are on a central computer so the agent will soon

know you are asking at other agencies. This will effectively destroy any mutually satisfying relationship you hoped to build. Looking for a compatible agent before you make plans is important. If, during the early planning stage, you decide to go elsewhere, be up-front. Tell the agent you are not happy and why.

If you go to more than one agency trying to get a better price on airline tickets, don't make reservations at each one. Booking airline tickets at more than one place can result in all reservations being canceled.

Be fair. If you want a trusting relationship for this vacation and future travel, you must be trustworthy, too.

A final touch

When you return home after your vacation, call your agent. Tell him or her what you enjoyed and what disappointed you.

A "thank you" card—perhaps even a souvenir—for a well planned trip is always appreciated.

Travel Agent's Check List

- ☐ Agent's Name _____
- ☐ Address _____
- ☐ Phone _____
- ☐ Fax _____
- ☐ E-mail _____
- ☐ Destination _____
- ☐ Transportation preference _____
- ☐ Agency fee _____
- ☐ Deposit made
- ☐ Reservations complete
- ☐ Final papers received
- ☐ Called agent after returning home.
- ☐

Chapter Nine

CUSTOMS

The U.S. Custom Service is the guardian of the nation's borders. They enforce the laws of the U.S., safeguard the revenue, and foster lawful international trade and travel.

Customs agents are mandated to treat you in a courteous, professional manner but are allowed to examine your baggage or vehicle, ask about your citizenship, your trip, and about anything you are bringing back to the United States that you did not have with you when you left.

If you need help clearing customs, do not hesitate to ask the Customs officer for help. They realize few travelers intend to break the law and are happy to help.

Several factors, such as recent terrorist attacks and threats, disease, and the attitude of the country toward foreigners will determine the extent of the inspection. For example, after the 9/11 attacks and the passing of the Patriot Act, U.S. customs became very restrictive and inspections increased dramatically.

Proof of purchase

Be sure you have proof of prior possession for valuable items such as cameras, watches, jewelry, and furs. The *best* proofs are the original receipts for each item. Insurance policies and jewelers' appraisals are also acceptable proof. Foreign-made items with serial numbers can be taken to a U.S. customs office for registration before you leave. Keep your receipts, appraisals, and registrations in a safe place. It is a good idea to make copies to leave at home with a friend or relative.

Medication

Be sure your medications are in order. Have the letters from your doctor available for inspectors if you have narcotics, needles, or syringes with you. Keep all prescription and over-the-counter medications in their original containers throughout your travel.

Don't make the same mistake as one businessman from San Diego. On his way home from an international trip, he dumped several medications in a small bag and threw away the original packaging because he wanted to save space in his luggage. U.S. customs delayed him for several hours while they identified what he was attempting to bring into the country.

Luckily, everything he had was legal. He could have been arrested for smuggling if customs had found any illegal (in the U.S.) drugs among his pills. Don't take foolish chances—drug smuggling is a serious offense.

Customs terms

- ‣ **Personal exemption.** Also called "duty-free exemption," it is the total value of merchandise you may bring back to the U.S. without having to pay duty. Depending on the countries you visited, your personal exemption may be $400, $600, or $1200. There are limits on the amount of cigarettes, cigars, other tobacco products, and alcoholic beverages you may include in your personal exemption.
- ‣ **Duty** is the amount of money you pay on items coming from another country. It is similar to a tax, except that duty is collected only on imported goods.
- ‣ **Dutiable** describes items on which duty may have to be paid.

▸ **Declare**. To "declare" means to tell the Customs officer about anything you are bringing into the country that you didn't have when you left.

Receipts

You will need receipts for all your foreign purchases. Keep them together in one place in your luggage or attach them to the purchased item.

Make sure you have the store's name and address, date of purchase, the item purchased, the total price, and the tax you paid on each receipt. Jot any missing information on the back of each receipt before you leave the store.

NOTE: Watch your purchases being wrapped at the store but unwrap them before packing in your suitcase to be sure you receive what you paid for and to be ready for customs inspection.

When you are doing your final packing before returning home, pin or tape the receipts on the items and try to keep the items together. Be sure you have receipts for items you are wearing, such as a watch or jewelry.

In the same place, keep the paper work for registered items.

Personal exemption and limits

There are some limits on what can be brought into the U.S. Tobacco and alcohol have quotas, for instance. You can bring in 100 cigars and 200 cigarettes and one liter of liquor for your own use or as a gift as part of your $400 exemption.

To qualify for the personal exemption, you must be out of the U.S. for at least 48 hours and not have claimed the exemption within the last 30 days.

The personal exemption is $400 with the following exceptions:

▸ Your exemption is $600 if you are returning directly from the following 24 Caribbean Basin counties: Antigua, Aruba, Bahamas, Barbados, Belize, Bermuda, British Virgin Islands, Costa Rica, Dominca, Dominican Republic, El Salvador, Granada, Guatemala, Guyana, Haiti, Honduras, Jamaica, Netherlands Antilles, Nicaragua, Panama, St. Kitts and Nevis, St. Lucia, St. Vincent and the Grenadines. You may bring in two liters of liquor if one of them was produced in any of the above countries.

▸ Your exemption is $1200 if you return, directly or indirectly, from a U.S. insular possession (U.S. Virgin islands, American Samoa, or Guam).

NOTE: Beware of shops or vendors trying to give you the wrong information. They may tell you the exemptions have increased or offer to give you receipts for less than you paid for the item. Don't do it! Customs officers are aware of the value of items. If caught, you, not the vendor, pay the penalty.

You may take personal belongings out of and into the country without paying customs and without the items counting as part of your duty-free allowance. This includes the following personal items with proof of origin:

▸ Vehicles for noncommercial use
▸ Household effects
▸ Tools of a trade

However, you will owe duty on any repairs or alterations to the above. Work done abroad on an item may change its duty status completely. For instance, if you take loose diamonds overseas to have them mounted, you will owe duty on the jewelry—including the value of the original diamonds — on its entire finished value. You can obtain detailed information about this aspect of customs law by contacting the U.S. Customs website.

Prohibited items

▶ Generally, **endangered species of wildlife**, and products made from them cannot be imported or exported. Ivory in any form has many restrictions. If you are even *thinking* of bringing back ivory, contact the Fish and Wildlife Service first. Turtle products, furs from endangered animals, and other animal derived items in any form are restricted by the U.S. and often the country of origin also. For detailed information contact the U.S. Fish and Wildlife Service, Division of Law Enforcement, 4401 North Fairfax Drive, Arlington VA 22203-3247. See their web site: *http://www.fws.gov* or call 800-358-2104.

▶ You may not bring back **fresh, dried, or canned meats**, or meat products from most foreign countries. Regulations may change frequently because they are based on disease outbreaks in different areas of the world.

▶ It is best not to try to bring home **fruits and vegetables**. Fresh fruits and vegetables can carry insects and diseases to U.S. The Mediterranean fruit fly was a hitchhiker on fruit brought into the country by a traveler. It cost the federal government and the state of California $100 million to get rid of it.

▶ **Plants, cuttings, seeds, unprocessed plant products**, and certain endangered species that are allowed in the U.S. require an import permit. *Every single plant* or plant product must be declared to the customs officer and presented for inspection, no matter how free of pests it appears to be.

Gifts

You may ship gifts worth $100 or less in fair retail value from abroad to the United States from the purchase point. One person cannot receive more than $100 in gift shipments per day. Gifts for more than one person can be sent in one container if they are individually wrapped and labeled inside and out with each recipient's name and address. Each gift may not exceed the $100 allowed value.

On the outside of the package, print **UNSOLICITED GIFT** and **CONSOLIDATED GIFT PACKAGE,** the contents, the total value of the contents, the recipients' names, and the nature and value of the gifts inside.

TIP: If you know you will be sending gifts from overseas, print labels with the wording above and separate labels with recipient's names and addresses. Then you only have to add the content and value information to the label before sticking it on your package.

You cannot send alcoholic beverages, tobacco products or perfume containing alcohol and worth more than five dollars.

The U.S. Postal Service sends all foreign mail shipments to Customs for examination. Customs then returns packages that don't require duty to the Postal Service. It sends them to the local post office for delivery. The local post office delivers them without charging any additional postage, handling costs, or other fees.

If the package requires payment of duty, Customs attaches a form called a "mail entry" form (CF-3419A) which shows how much duty is owed and charges a $5 processing fee as well. When the post office delivers the package, they also charge a fee.

NOTE: If any one item in the gift package is valued at more than the $100 allowed, the entire package becomes dutiable.

Duty on items you mail to yourself will be waived if the value is $200 or less. Fine art and antiques over 100 years old are duty exempt.

Gifts you carry through customs are included as part of your total exemption.

Gifts for commercial purposes are not duty-free.

Pets and other animals

If you plan to take your pet abroad or import one on your return, please get a copy of Customs booklet, *Pets, Wildlife, U.S. Customs.* It not only has important information about the legal aspects of the issue, it will also save you a lot of hassles. In addition, check with state, county, and local authorities to learn if their restrictions and prohibitions on pets are stricter than the federal requirement.

Importing animals is closely regulated for public health reasons and also for the well-being of the animals There are restrictions and prohibitions on bringing many species into the United States.

If you decide to take a pet, be sure it is checked by a veterinarian and all shots are current. Carry the pet in an airline approved carrier.

Better yet, leave the pet at home with a safe caretaker. You may both be happier.

Paying duty

Upon your return to the United States, you must pay required duty on the items you have acquired overseas. Your allowed exemption is deducted from the total value of the items before duty is calculated. You may pay your duty with:

- United States Currency
- Personal check in the exact amount of duty. The check must be drawn on a national or state bank or trust company of the United States and made payable to U.S. Customs Service. No two-party checks are accepted.
- Government check, money order, or travelers' check if it does not exceed the duty owed by more than $50.
- In some locations, you may pay duty with MasterCard or Visa credit cards.
- Duty cannot be prepaid

NOTE: *Send for the customs booklet, Know Before You Go, listed in the Resource Section or log on to www.customs.gov and click on "Traveler Information."*

Foreign country regulations

Call the embassies or consulates of the countries you plan to visit for current information about their regulations. Don't forget to check with the embassies of countries which you will be traveling *through.*

If you have to drive, ride a bus or train through a country to get to your destination country, you must meet the regulations of the country traveled through or they can stop you at the border. Of course, if you are flying over a country, this is not a concern.

When you check a country's regulations, you may be surprised by what is illegal. For instance, books or magazines with pictures of scantily clad women are forbidden in Moslem countries.

Kudos

Give Customs officials the respect they deserve. Their expertise has stopped terrorists, led to the confiscation of drugs, and kept criminals and other *personas non grata* out of the country. They are a solid line of protection for all U.S. citizens.

Chapter Ten

LUGGAGE

While traveling light, you will usually need three pieces of luggage: a suitcase, carry-on bag and purse or waist pack. Your luggage should be of good quality but not lavish or obviously expensive. For example, an embossed fine leather suitcase is a magnet for thieves, including airline and airport employees.

Suitcase

Samsonite, American Tourister, Global Traveler, Skyway, and Travelpro, among others, make sturdy, dependable luggage.

For example, Samsonite makes *Estes EZ Cart* with a huge main compartment and an exterior front pocket. It can be pushed or pulled by its retractable handles. The wheels are big and partly recessed so they travel safely in baggage compartments. Its retail price is about $200 but you can find it at outlets and on sale discounted as much as 50%.

In many countries, including the U.S., you may find it necessary to maneuver long walks or flights of stairs with your luggage. Often, no porters are available. I strongly advise you to take a suitcase with wheels and a handle. The handle should be long enough so you don't have to stoop while pulling it.

NOTE: Magellan's Travel Supply has an extension handle to add length to suitcase handles. Great for tall persons.

Some suitcases have a strap to secure your carry-on bag on top. Choose one with a secure strap. It's a hassle if the carry-on bag slips or falls off repeatedly.

NOTE: Always push your luggage in front of you when you have your carry-on strapped to it.

Soft-sided suitcases are less likely to suffer damage if dropped or thrown. In addition, they are expandable.

Look through stores, ask the advice of the salesperson. Check the insides of bags and wheel them around to make sure they roll easily and are comfortable for your height. Are the zippers sturdy? Do they open and close easily? Be sure you can put a lock on the zippers. Shop early and look for sales. Luckily, luggage is frequently on sale at major department stores.

A bag 24" x 16" x 7 ½" is a good size for one person. You will have plenty of room for everything you need to be comfortable *and* well dressed.

Investing in an expandable carry-on bag means you won't have to wait for your baggage when you arrive at your destination. On a weekend trip or short business trip, it makes sense to use a carry-on bag because you won't have much with you. Travelpro makes garment bags that fold up into a convenient size so you can stow them under a seat. It folds to 20" x 22" x 3", expands to 42", has hanger clamps and zippered, see-through compartments everywhere.

Travelpro's "5-Pocket Tote" has all sorts of spacious compartments and pockets. It attaches to their roll-around bags three different ways. Size is 15" x 11" x 8 ½" and weight is only 1½ pounds when empty.

NOTE: Some travelers choose to travel very light with only carry-on baggage. Decide what works best for you. My personal choice on a long vacation is to check my larger bag. I don't like lugging all my things through airports, then trying to stuff them into overhead bins or under a seat on the plane. I look forward to checking in my one large bag and having only my carry-on and purse to keep track of in the airport. Another point to think about—if the plane bins are too full, you'll end up checking your bag anyway.

Carry-on bag

Carry-on bags should have a sturdy strap, zipper closures and be small enough to fit under the seat of a plane. If you are buying a new one, choose one made of heavy, textured nylon. Since you will have it with you during much of your travels, be sure the strap is wide, comfortable, and short enough so the bag hangs no farther than your waist when the strap is on your shoulder. Try to find one with separate, zippered compartments, one of them vinyl lined.

Travelpro's "5-Pocket Tote" is expensive. However, even if you do a lot of traveling, you will probably never have to buy a new one.

Purse

A purse has always been a woman traveler's best friend.

The ideal purse is no deeper than 8 ½" and no longer than 16". It has a soft bottom that expands to five inches when crammed full but is less than one inch when empty. Look for one with a fold-over flap and/or a top zipper for each of two main compartments. The purse you choose should have two strong straps just long enough so you can place the purse securely under your upper arm. A purse made of soft, ripple leather that doesn't show scratches is a good choice. Try to find one with a distinctive design element (for example, a zipper pull in an animal shape)for easy identification. Choose a purse in your main color. (see next chapter)

An easily accessible outside, open pocket is handy for carrying an umbrella, maps, and guidebooks. *(See designed-for-travelers purses at travel supply companies in Resource Section)*

Waist bag

Men, women, and children appreciate the convenience of waist bags. You keep your hands free and you don't have to worry about misplacing it. Men have somewhere besides their pockets to carry necessities. Women and children use them to carry essentials—small amounts of cash, medicine, tissues, and a few other necessities—when going shopping or on a walking tour. You can strap a water bottle to it if you need one.

Find waist bags made especially for travelers at travel supply stores. *(see list in Resource Section)* or make your own from several patterns in books.

NOTE: Foil thieves and avoid accidental breakage by buying or making a waist bag with a sturdy strap and a substantial belt and buckle rather a velcro fastening. Always wear the pack in front or to the side. Carry your passport, credit cards, keys, and most of your cash in a security pouch worn around your neck or waist and inside your clothing.

Attach a label with your name, address, phone number, and contact person's name and phone number to the inside of your and your children's waist packs.

Backpacks

Increasingly popular for travelers. If you are doing a lot of sightseeing or walking about the countryside, you can carry all you need yet keep your hands free. Extra clothing, bad weather gear, water, snacks, first aid kits, and medication, can all be easily carried. Buy a well-constructed pack with a zippered closure and lock. Try it on and adjust the straps for comfort before you buy.

Wearing a backpack used to identify the wearer as a tourist but now they are so universally used, they are not as conspicuous. They have been used to carry terrorist bombs so expect it to be searched by authorities when you board planes, buses, trains, and subways.

Security pouches

Security pouches are soft cloth, flat bags to wear under your clothing. They enable you to carry valuables out of reach of pickpockets and "snatch and run" thieves. Some tuck inside your belt, some you wear attached to a bra and some hang around your neck inside your clothing. (Tuck cord out of sight, too.) Buy them from travel supply stores or make your own. *(see Resource Section).*

Luggage Tags

Attach a sturdy luggage tag to your suitcase, carry-on, purse, and waist bag. Buy one with a protective cover so a casual observer can't see your name or address.

TIP: Do something different! Insert a picture of a loved one in the tag. Write your name and address on the back of the picture or on a separate card and out of sight. You will instantly recognize the picture and you can show the name and address if airport security requires it.

Locks

Airline personnel now have the right by law to look inside your luggage even when it is out of your sight. If they choose your bag to inspect, they may break the lock unless you have a Travel Sentry™ Certified Lock. This is a special lock certified by the TSA. It enables airport security to access the contents of your suitcase with secured tools that do not damage the locks. You can also use disposable luggage seals. (*See Magellan's Travel Supply in Resource Section*)

Quick Identification

Tie two or three bright colored pieces of yarn or ribbon around the handles of your luggage or stick on a colorful decal to help you spot your bags on the carousel. It is still necessary to check your luggage tags for your identification.

Luggage List

☐ Suitcase

☐ Releaseable strap for suitcase

☐ Carry-on bag

☐ Purse

☐ Waist pack

☐ Backpack

☐ Security pouch

☐ Luggage tags

☐ TSA Certified locks or disposable luggage seals *(see travel supply companies in Resource Section)*

Chapter Eleven

CHOOSING CLOTHING

The first, and often only, consideration inexperienced travelers give to clothing is, "How will it look?" The more you travel, the more you know about other important issues that come into play when choosing clothing.

A major contribution to your pleasure—or lack of same—when you travel is how you choose to react to meeting new people with customs different from your own. If you blunder in and show by your words and attitude you think your. ways are the only correct ones, you will offend people and spoil your vacation. The truth is, you will enjoy yourself more if you respect people and their customs.

NOTE: My experience when meeting people in different countries is that if you show friendliness and a lively curiosity about their country, you will receive friendliness in return.

This respect extends to clothing and behavior. Customs related to dress can be an intrinsic part of a country's religion or what they consider proper dress for men and women.

This doesn't mean you don a *burka* in Moslem countries. It does mean you dress modestly in sleeved dresses or in pants with long tunics. If you insist on wearing shorts, miniskirts, bare midriff or sleeveless clothing, you may be insulted or even injured. That's no fun!

In European countries, don't wear shorts, mini-skirts and "barely there" tops to cathedrals, shrines, the theater or opera and fine restaurants. The people in charge will not allow you to enter. Save your revealing clothing for the beach or pool-side. Learn about the customs of the countries you will visit. You and the country's citizens will feel more comfortable. After reading about them, if you find you are too unhappy with the customs of a country, perhaps you need to reconsider going there.

The climate and season in the places you visit should also influence the clothing you choose. Find out about the weather from travel agents, tourist boards, weather bureaus, books, magazines, and the Internet. Realize the temperature may be many degrees warmer or colder at any given time than the average temperature.

Remember to consider any special health issues that may affect what you need to wear.

The best way to dress in any climate is layering. Two or three layers of clothing are more comfortable than a single bulky coat or sweater. Air is trapped between the layers and warmed by your body heat to keep you warm.

Picture yourself on a cold, spring morning. You will be outdoors all day so you decide to wear woolen pants, a bulky sweater with an undershirt, and heavy socks with your walking shoes. You are warm and cosy until about 11 a.m. Then you become too warm, sweaty, and remain uncomfortable for the rest of the day.

Or, you choose a long-sleeved cotton shirt, a button-up polar-fleece vest and a long, lightweight cardigan. You have on two pairs of lightweight socks (one pair knee length) and cotton pants. As the day warms up, you take off the vest, the extra socks, and the cardigan, and roll up the sleeves of your shirt. Folded small, the surplus garments can be tied to your waist or go into your backpack if you have one. You are comfortable all day.

On other occasions during your travel, each of the garments in the second scenario can be mixed and matched with other items in your wardrobe. Layering gives you comfort *and* versatility.

Care of the clothing you bring is important to consider. A pure linen pantsuit may be a "hot" fashion but you'll feel like throwing it in the trash when you have to take care of it during your travel.

Wrinkle resistant, washable fabric is great for your travel wardrobe. Micro knits and a fortrel-cotton blends are ideal fabrics. You can fold them, crumple them, or sit on them and they seldom wrinkle. They are easy to wash and dry quickly. Washable knits, crinkle weaves, cotton sheeting, and silky synthetic crepes also travel well.

TIP: *Check out the easy-care travel clothes in the TravelSmith catalog. (see Resource Section).*

Wash your clothes the way you will be washing them on your trip. You'll know for sure how they will look while you travel. Many good hotels will furnish you with an ironing board and an iron if you must press. You can also order valet service—usually at a high cost.

Versatile garments you can dress up or down are the basics of your travel wardrobe. You don't always have to choose blouses, jackets, and skirts. An interesting garment is a princess style or chemise style dress made of wrinkle-proof, easy wash fabric. Choose a simple neckline, long or elbow length sleeves and below knee length in your main wardrobe color. *(More about that later.)*

Wear it in the evening with a faux jeweled collar and a chiffon shawl or fasten on a jeweled belt and a lamé vest or top the dress with a sheer, glittery overdress. Change its look by a variety of scarves, jewelry, belts, vests, and jackets so you can wear it any time of the day for almost any occasion. The dress and the accessories take up little room in your suitcase.

Changeable climates in Britain and Scandinavian countries make taking a coat necessary. Choose a raincoat with a warm, zip-out lining and removable hood in a color to match or contrast with one of the main two colors in your travel wardrobe. A high quality coat will look good during the whole trip. Look for wrinkle-proof fabric. Plan to wear it on the plane. Depending on the weather, wear it with or without the lining. Don't forget to take an umbrella!

Another versatile garment is the tee shirt. Young people around the world are as fond of their jeans and tee shirts as their counterparts in the U.S. Try to find some in a fabric blend or a treated pure cotton fiber to cut down on wrinkling. Instead of throwing in every shirt you have, choose carefully so they will mix and match with your chosen colors and accessory items such as vests, jackets, and scarves.

TIP: If you sew, make your basic dress or dresses. If not, have one made by a dressmaker. You may not be able to find the style and color you want in a store. TravelSmith sells one in different lengths in several colors. (As this book goes to print, these basic dresses can be found in a variety of colors in many stores and catalogs.)

A consistent color scheme simplifies your planning. Ask yourself, "What is my most flattering color?" Make it the color you build your wardrobe around. Chances are you already have several travel-ready garments in this color.

Choose carefully. You want to be able to mix and match almost everything for a variety of looks without a ton of clothing. Non-patterned garments are most versatile. Add patterns with vests and scarves.

Opt for familiar colors. If you always wear black or beige but want to experiment with bright colors, choose black or beige as your main color and add splashes of bright colors with your contrast and accent colors.

Make sure your clothes fit well and the fabrics are comfortable next to your skin. Scratchy material will not become easier to wear on vacation.

Have you ever gone to a party wearing clothing in a color or style in which you feel uncomfortable? The inner perception that you don't look your best influences your reaction to the entire party. Feeling comfortable with your clothing choices is an important aspect of enjoying your travel.

TIP: Choose clothes with usable pockets whenever you can. They are handy for carrying small items, such as change.

DON'T TAKE

BULKY SWEATERS: They take up too much room. Layered lightweight clothing is better.

HEAVY SHOES OR BOOTS: There are many light support shoes available.

CLOTHES THAT WRINKLE EASILY: More trouble than they are worth.

VALUABLE FURS, JEWELRY, CAMERAS, WATCHES: They make you a highly visible target for thieves.

BREAKABLE BOTTLES: Why risk a mess and maybe a cut hand when plastic containers are cheap and unbreakable?

PRESSURIZED SPRAY CONTAINER: Not only can they explode at high altitudes, they are illegal on planes.

ANYTHING ILLEGAL: Drugs, endangered species items, weapons, liquor, and sexually oriented material are among the forbidden items in some countries. Know before you go.

No matter where you go, chances are you will be walking a lot. Take comfortable, well fitting shoes—this is not the place to economize. If you are buying new shoes, wear them several times to be sure they are comfortable and provide support to your feet. Wear them at different times of the day since feet tend to swell in the afternoon.

Sports shoes designed for walking are good but may not always coordinate with your clothes. Women can buy a basic pump with a 1" to 1½" heel in their main color to wear with skirts and dresses. Buy some elegant clips or bows to dress them up for evening.

Cruise clothes

Cruising wardrobes are a challenge because you have three categories of activities: shipboard day activities, shipboard evening activities, and shore excursions. The formality of each activity depends on the cruise. Windjammer or small boat Alaska cruises will require no special evening attire while a cruise on a Cunard line ship may require formal or semi-formal dress every evening. Yes, you can look elegant *and* travel light.

On cruises where you need formal clothing, the basic dress (described earlier) can be dressed up for formal occasions. Buy or make one in a medium or long length, sleeveless or with short or cape sleeves and a lowered neckline. With very little room taken up in your suitcase, you can have many outfits. Some ideas:

▸ Add a sequined or lamé vest, necklace, and a belt.
▸ Make or buy a flowing, chiffon tunic to wear over the dress.
▸ Wear an eye-catching necklace and a bright lace or chiffon shawl over your shoulders.

Other options for evening attire include one or two full skirts, one in your main color and one in your main contrast. For more versatility, choose mid-calf length in soft, silky, non-shiny fabrics. Buy a variety of vests, blouses, scarves, and jewelry in your colors. Magic! Dozens of outfits all in only one suitcase.

Most people on a cruise dress for dinner. However, the elaborate display of gowns and tuxedos you see on television aren't necessary. Men can choose to wear a tuxedo, of course, but a regular suit is perfectly acceptable.

The mid-calf length skirts can be worn with different tops during daytime shore excursions. You will be appropriately dressed for almost any situation. With the skirt, wear:

▸ A peasant style blouse, a bright belt, and a straw hat with a ribbon band or big, silk flower. Comfortable, colorful sandals on your feet and a canvas or straw bag to carry and you are ready for sightseeing in most ports. You are dressed properly to sightsee, shop and sample the local food.
▸ Add a jacket, a simple blouse, a necklace, stockings, and basic shoes to the skirt and you are ready for business meetings, visits to shrines or churches, or even a visit with the Pope!

Daytime shipboard activities are usually casual. One or two well-fitting bathing suits, shorts, long pants, tops, a sun hat, a matching carryall and sandals are the basics. All should be in your colors. Bermuda shorts or long pants can be worn with tops on shore excursions, too.

NOTE: Sun hats with an all-around brim are more efficient in keeping the sun off your head and neck than front-billed caps. A straw hat gives you good ventilation. Buy one at a local market, use for the cruise, then give it away. Or you can buy a fabric hat that folds easily. (TravelSmith catalog has several.)

Color choice
Give thought to your color choices. You know the colors most flattering to your complexion. As you plan your trip, pick out one Main Color (MC) one Main Contrasting Color (MCC), two accent colors (AC1 and AC2). A third accent color can be metallic gold or silver.

Before you buy anything, look at the clothes you already own.
- Do you have suitable garments in a favorite color? What color? _____
- Scarves? _____
- Costume jewelry_____
- Shawls _____
- Shoes, handbags _____

Lay the suitable clothes out on the bed. Mix and match. Then use the clothes lists on the following pages to decide what you need to buy.

Remember these are *suggestions*. Nothing is carved in stone. The lists have been compiled from personal travel, the experiences of others and printed resources.

Use the checklists to make packing lists. Think about what you want to do. Which items are appropriate for the activity. If some items on lists are not your style, don't use them. This is your vacation!

Color Chart

MC		MCC		AC-1		AC-2		AC-3	
Black		Lime		Yellow		Coral		Gold	
Black		Red		Yellow		White		Silver	
Black		Grey		Pink		White		Silver	
Brown		Aqua		Yellow		Coral		Gold	
Brown		Yellow		Pink		Cream		Gold	
Brown		Beige		Yellow		Cream		Gold	
Beige		Cream		Red		Lt. blue		Gold	
Beige		Peach		Aqua		Brown		Gold	
Green		Lt. Grn.		Orchid		Cream		Gold	
Grey		Dk.Gold		White		Red		Silver	
Dk. Blue		Lt. Blue		Peach		White		Silver	
Khaki		Red		Yellow		White		Gold	
Olive		Orchid		Pink		White		Gold	
Red		Blue		Yellow		White		Silver	
Grey		Yellow		Red		Black		Silver	

MC = Main Color, MCC = Main Contrast Color,

AC-1, AC-2 = Accent colors, AC-3 = metallic accent

NOTE: Fill in the boxes next to the color names on the chart with colored pencils.
Or, send an e-mail to joyn0429@sbcglobal.net to request a color chart

Clothing Lists
Women—Europe—Summer

Suggested Fabrics: Cotton blends, crepes, silky blends, knits

Main Color _____

- ☐ Skirt
- ☐ Long pants
- ☐ Tailored shorts
- ☐ Jacket
- ☐ Blouse
- ☐ Basic dress
- ☐ Shoes, comfortable for walking
- ☐ Handbag

Main Contrast Color _____

- ☐ Skirt
- ☐ Long pants
- ☐ Tailored shorts
- ☐ Jacket
- ☐ Blouse
- ☐ Long dress or skirt
- ☐ Vest

Accent 1 _____

- ☐ Skirt
- ☐ Pants
- ☐ Blouse or tee shirt
- ☐ Cardigan
- ☐ Vest
- ☐ Scarf

- ☐ Belt
- ☐ Necklaces and earrings

Accent 2 _____

- ☐ Skirt
- ☐ Pants
- ☐ Blouse or tee shirt
- ☐ Vest
- ☐ Belt
- ☐ Scarf
- ☐ Evening shawl
- ☐ Necklaces, earrings

Accent 3 (Gold or Silver) _____

- ☐ Evening bag
- ☐ Dressy sandals or shoes
- ☐ Belt
- ☐ Vest
- ☐ Necklaces and earrings

Other

- ☐ Nightgown or pajamas
- ☐ Robe (lightweight, opaque)
- ☐ Slippers
- ☐ Raincoat (folds up into a small package)
- ☐ Rain hat
- ☐ Folding umbrella
- ☐ Five sets of underwear
- ☐ One or two non-cling slips
- ☐ Five pair stockings
- ☐ Five pair socks

☐ Bathing suit
☐ Cover up (use one of your blouses or bathrobe)
☐ Poolside sandals
☐ Foldable sun hat

Women—Europe—Spring, Fall

Fabrics: Wool blends, crepes, knits, cotton blends

Main Color _____

- ☐ Skirt
- ☐ Long pants
- ☐ Jacket, blazer type
- ☐ Dress
- ☐ Blouse
- ☐ Pullover sweater in lightweight knit or silk
- ☐ Shoes
- ☐ All weather coat with zip out lining

Main Contrast Color _____

- ☐ Skirt
- ☐ Pants
- ☐ Jacket, casual with hood
- ☐ Blouse
- ☐ Vest
- ☐ Shoes
- ☐ Warm hat
- ☐ Gloves

Accent 1 _____

- ☐ Skirt or pants
- ☐ Tee shirt
- ☐ Cardigan sweater
- ☐ Vest
- ☐ Scarf
- ☐ Shawl, warm but not bulky for day or evening

- ☐ Necklace, earrings
- ☐ Belt

Accent 2 _____

- ☐ Skirt or pants
- ☐ Blouse, tee shirt or knit shirt
- ☐ Vest
- ☐ Scarf
- ☐ Cardigan sweater (Lightweight wool)
- ☐ Necklace, earrings
- ☐ Belt

Accent 3 (Gold or Silver) _____

- ☐ Belt
- ☐ Evening handbag
- ☐ Vest
- ☐ Blouse
- ☐ Shoes

Other

- ☐ Nightgown or pajamas (warm, modest)
- ☐ Robe, lightweight but warm
- ☐ Bed socks
- ☐ Folding umbrella
- ☐ Five sets underwear
- ☐ Long underwear (top and bottom in all silk are warm and take up minimal room. (Damart sells them)
- ☐ One or two non-cling slips
- ☐ Five pair stockings
- ☐ Five pair of socks

Put it together

How do you put it all together? In the following examples, one garment, the main color skirt, from a color scheme of brown, tan, yellow, turquoise and silver is featured. The fabrics are crepes and knits for summer travel in Europe.

Example 1
- Brown crepe, mid-knee length, gored skirt with a flared hem and a flat elastic waistband.
- Brown crepe blouse with short sleeves and a round neckline.
- A yellow, flat-knit cardigan and a yellow chiffon scarf around your neck.
- Brown shoes and your handbag.

Example 2:
- Brown skirt (same as above)
- Brown blazer.
- Tan blouse – Crepe, short sleeved with V neckline.
- Turquoise and yellow bead necklaces.
- Turquoise earrings.
- Brown shoes, and handbag

Both of these outfits are appropriate for shopping, enjoying luncheons or breakfasts, or sightseeing in churches, museums and gardens. When the weather warms up, you can remove the sweater or jacket and still look well dressed.

Example 3
- Brown skirt (same as above).
- Crepe turquoise, V-necked, button-up blouse with peplum.

- Turquoise shawl.
- Silver necklace and earrings.
- Silver bag and shoes

Example 4
- Brown skirt
- Silver lamé, button-up, lined vest with a low neckline and crystal or rhinestone buttons
- Silver earrings
- Turquoise shawl
- Silver bag and shoes

These two outfits are elegant and festive for dinner, theater, concerts, and parties.

These are just some of the outfits you can put together starting with only one of the basic garments.

Your own taste and imagination help you choose the clothing and the colors flattering to your complexion and your figure. You can travel light and be elegantly dressed, too.

Men—Europe—Summer

Fabrics: Cotton blends and knits
Main color _____
- ☐ Suit
- ☐ Sport shirt
- ☐ Casual trousers
- ☐ Shoes (dress)
- ☐ Socks (dress)
- ☐ Shorts
- ☐ Belt

Main Contrast Color _____
- ☐ Sport jacket
- ☐ Sport shirt
- ☐ Shorts
- ☐ Casual trousers

Contrast Color 1 _____
- ☐ Cardigan sweater
- ☐ Sport shirt or tee shirt
- ☐ Print sport shirt
- ☐ Casual trousers
- ☐ Shorts

Contrast Color 2 _____
- ☐ Windbreaker type jacket
- ☐ Sport shirt
- ☐ Tee shirt
- ☐ Trousers
- ☐ Shorts

☐ Tie
Other
☐ Dress shirt (white)
☐ Dress shirt (white)
☐ Pajamas
☐ Robe (Lightweight cotton)
☐ Foldup slippers
☐ Bathing suit
☐ Rubber flip-flop sandals
☐ Walking shoes
☐ Walking shoes
☐ Five sets of underwear
☐ Five pair casual socks
☐ Belts or suspenders
☐ Foldup raincoat
☐ Umbrella
☐ Jeans

TIP: Europeans dress conservatively.

Men—Europe—Fall, Spring

Fabrics: Wool blends, dacron blends, knits
Main Color _____
- ☐ Suit
- ☐ Sport shirt
- ☐ Casual trousers
- ☐ Pullover sweater
- ☐ All-weather coat with zip out lining
- ☐ Shoes (dress)

Main Contrast Color _____
- ☐ Sport jacket
- ☐ Sport shirt
- ☐ Casual trousers
- ☐ Dress shirt
- ☐ Cardigan sweater
- ☐ Warm hat
- ☐ Walking shoes
- ☐ Gloves

Accent 1 _____
- ☐ Sport shirt
- ☐ Tee shirt or polo shirt
- ☐ Casual trousers
- ☐ Windbreaker jacket
- ☐ Tie

Accent 2 _____
- ☐ Sport shirt

☐ Tee shirt or polo shirt
☐ Tie

Other

☐ Five sets underwear (undershirts *and* shorts)
☐ Five pair socks
☐ Pajamas
☐ Robe (Flannel is lightweight and warm)
☐ Slipper socks
☐ Umbrella
☐ Waterproof shoe covers
☐ Long underwear (Silk Damart™ underwear is warm)
☐ Belts or suspenders

Women—Hot Climates

Fabrics: Choose gauze, cotton plissé, pants-weight gauze, sheeting, microfiber knits

Main Color _____
- ☐ Skirt
- ☐ Pants
- ☐ Shorts
- ☐ Tee shirt
- ☐ Blouse
- ☐ Dress
- ☐ Shawl (Air-conditioned buildings can get chilly.)
- ☐ Walking shoes
- ☐ Sandals

Main Contrast Color _____
- ☐ Skirt
- ☐ Pants or shorts
- ☐ Dress
- ☐ Tee shirt or blouse
- ☐ Tank top or halter

Accent 1 _____
- ☐ Pants or skirt
- ☐ Shorts
- ☐ Blouse
- ☐ Tank top, tee shirt or halter
- ☐ Cardigan (light weight)
- ☐ Necklace and earrings

Accent 2 _____

- ☐ Pants or skirt
- ☐ Shorts
- ☐ Blouse
- ☐ Tank top or tee shirt
- ☐ Earrings and necklace

Accent 3 (Gold or Silver) _____

- ☐ Belt
- ☐ Sandals
- ☐ Handbag
- ☐ Evening blouse or vest
- ☐ Necklace and earrings

Other

- ☐ Nightgown or pajamas
- ☐ Robe
- ☐ Swimsuit
- ☐ Swimsuit
- ☐ Coverup
- ☐ Poolside sandals
- ☐ Five sets underwear
- ☐ One non-cling slip or half-slip
- ☐ Socks to wear with walking shoes
- ☐ Stockings (optional)
- ☐ Belts
- ☐ Scarf to pull back hair
- ☐ Brimmed, open-weave hat

Men—Hot Climates and Cruises

Fabrics - Cotton blend, loose weave knits

- ☐ Suit - Summer weight
- ☐ Short sleeved dress shirt
- ☐ Short sleeved dress shirt
- ☐ Sport shirt (loose weave cotton)
- ☐ Sport shirt
- ☐ Sport shirt
- ☐ Tank top, tee shirt or polo shirt
- ☐ Tank top, tee shirt or polo shirt
- ☐ Tank top, tee shirt or polo shirt
- ☐ Shorts
- ☐ Shorts
- ☐ Shorts
- ☐ Casual pants or jeans
- ☐ Casual pants
- ☐ Cardigan sweater
- ☐ Windbreaker jacket
- ☐ Sports jacket
- ☐ Dress shoes
- ☐ Sandals
- ☐ Tennis shoes
- ☐ Belts
- ☐ Five sets underwear
- ☐ Pajamas
- ☐ Robe

- ☐ Five pair socks
- ☐ Bathing suit
- ☐ Bathing suit
- ☐ Poolside sandals
- ☐ Cover up

Choose three colors to coordinate your clothes, such as
- ☐ Dark blue, light blue, yellow
- ☐ Dark gray, light gray, red
- ☐ Beige, dark green, light orange
- ☐ Brown, beige, yellow
- ☐ _____ _____ _____

WOMEN – CRUISE

Fabrics: washable crepes, gauzes, cotton blends, silky blends. Washable wool, warm knits for cold climate cruising.

Main color _____

- ☐ Shorts* or long pants
- ☐ Shorts* or long pants
- ☐ Skirt* √ (crepe, full, below knee length or long)
- ☐ Skirt (sporty style)
- ☐ Blouse
- ☐ Tee shirt, polo shirt
- ☐ Halter* or vest that can be worn alone
- ☐ Sandals* (walking type)
- ☐ Shawl
- ☐ Dress √ (basic style)

Main contrast color _____

- ☐ Shorts* or long pants
- ☐ Skirt* √ (lined voile or crepe georgette)
- ☐ Blouse
- ☐ Tee shirt or polo shirt
- ☐ Cardigan sweater
- ☐ Vest √

Accent 1 _____

- ☐ Shorts*
- ☐ Pants
- ☐ Blouse (peasant style)
- ☐ Tee shirt or polo shirt
- ☐ Vest or halter* √ (embroidered or brocade)
- ☐ Necklace and earrings

Accent 2 _____
- ☐ Chiffon scarf
- ☐ Shorts*
- ☐ Blouse
- ☐ Tank top or halter*
- ☐ Chiffon shawl* √
- ☐ Necklace and earrings*

Accent 3 (metallic) _____
- ☐ Sandals* √
- ☐ Evening bag* √
- ☐ Vest* √
- ☐ Blouse* √
- ☐ Belt* √
- ☐ Necklace and earrings* √

Other
- ☐ Swimsuit
- ☐ Swimsuit*
- ☐ Cover up
- ☐ Pool side sandals (Use as slippers, too)
- ☐ Workout clothes √
- ☐ Pajamas or nightgown
- ☐ Robe (Optional)
- ☐ Five sets underwear
- ☐ Tennis shoes
- ☐ Socks
- ☐ Stockings
- ☐ Straw hat*

This entire list is for a cruise on a large ship in a warm climate with formal events, shore excursions in ports and daytime activities on shipboard.

✓ Modify the list if you are going to be cruising on a Windjammer, or small ship cruising by eliminating the checked (✓) items

* Skip the starred items if you are cruising to Alaska or other cold climates. Add a jacket, hats, gloves, socks, warm underwear and closed shoes. Take only one skirt.

Add list
☐ Jacket (Polar Fleece)
☐ Hat (warm and covers ears)
☐ Gloves
☐ Socks
☐ Warm shoes
☐ Waterproof covers for shoes
☐ Rain gear
☐ Long underwear

Chapter Twelve

GROOMING AND OTHER ESSENTIALS

Think compact. Eight ounce plastic containers will usually give you plenty of shampoo, conditioner and lotions for a seven to ten day trip. After you choose your colors, choose the makeup to complement them—and you!

Organize your grooming items by category. In separate reclosable plastic bags pack the following.

▸ Day makeup
▸ Evening makeup
▸ Manicure necessities
▸ Items you take into the shower
▸ Hair care items

Schedule appointments for the following to help you look your best. It will give you confidence in unfamiliar situations. Choose the items that apply to you.

☐ Schedule a haircut, trim and perm (if you usually perm your hair) a couple of weeks before you leave
☐ Have a professional manicure and pedicure a couple of days before you leave
☐ Color your hair
☐ Have your legs and bikini line waxed

LIST OF GROOMING ITEMS AND OTHER ESSENTIALS

- ☐ Hand lotion
- ☐ Body lotion
- ☐ Face Cream
- ☐ Moisturizer
- ☐ Shaving Cream
- ☐ Disposable razors
- ☐ Shampoo
- ☐ Conditioner
- ☐ Small reclosable plastic bag of cotton swabs
- ☐ Small reclosable plastic bag of cotton balls
- ☐ Makeup remover pads
- ☐ Reclosable plastic bag with hairpins and curlers
- ☐ Wash cloth or two (many European countries don't have them in hotels) in a reclosable plastic bag.
- ☐ Large reclosable (2 ½ gallon) plastic bags (6)
- ☐ Shower cap
- ☐ Toothpaste
- ☐ Toothbrush
- ☐ Dental floss
- ☐ Bar soap in soap dish (one bar for each seven days of travel)
- ☐ Travel size hair dryer
- ☐ Curling iron
- ☐ Cold water wash for clothes
- ☐ Sunscreen (at least 15 SPF)
- ☐ Tweezers
- ☐ Mirror in case*

Nail care (keep it simple)
- ☐ Emery boards or file
- ☐ Clippers

Other
- ☐ Sewing kit
- ☐ 16 packages of pocket size tissue. One in purse*
- ☐ Sunglasses*
- ☐ Comb*
- ☐ Brush*
- ☐ Deodorant
- ☐ Mouthwash
- ☐ Feminine hygiene supplies
- ☐ Birth control
- ☐ Eyeglass repair kit
- ☐ Contact lens care
- ☐ Hair accessories—scrunchies, barrettes, scarves
- ☐ Lip balm*

Makeup in reclosable plastic bag
- ☐ Brushes
- ☐ Eye shadow
- ☐ Eyeliner
- ☐ Mascara
- ☐ Eyebrow makeup
- ☐ Foundation*
- ☐ Powder
- ☐ Lip liner and lipstick*
- ☐ _____
- ☐ _____

Emergency and miscellaneous supplies
- ☐ Clothesline and pins

☐ Swiss army knife* (can't take on planes)
☐ String bag for shopping
☐ Earplugs*
☐ Flashlight* (small, travel size)
☐ Travel alarm clock
☐ Travel pillow* (flat—fill with air when you use it.)
☐ Slipper socks
☐ Travel reading light
☐ Currency converter
☐ Books*
☐ Plastic laundry bag
☐ Tampons
☐ Sanitary pads
☐ Stamps and postcards
☐ Pens*
☐ Maps*
☐ Guidebooks*
☐ Metric measuring tape
☐ Mailing labels
☐ Two sets batteries for camera, flashlight
☐ Film
☐ Camera
☐ Travel diary*
☐ X-ray proof film pouch. (Heavy and awkward. Check if you can carry your film and have it hand inspected instead.)
☐ Umbrella (if necessary for the climate)
☐ Adaptor plug set for electrical items (Travel stores and www.magellans.com)

☐ Binoculars*. Purchase the best you can afford. Enhances viewing of natural settings such as, animals, birds, scenery details, building details, and more

* Items to pack in your purse. Most of the other items on this list will be packed in your carry-on

Camera notes

You may hate an expensive camera with lots of lenses and gadgets before you return from your vacation. Leave it at home. In addition to the inconvenience of dragging it around, it will be a target for thieves.

Check out small cameras you can carry in a pocket. They take beautiful pictures almost automatically. You can purchase a small, light camera with telescopic lenses, automatic focusing, flash attachment in the camera and other amenities.

Digital cameras allow you to screen your pictures so you can print only the shots you like. Good ones (3 or 4 pixel) are expensive but the price is coming down.

Talk to a person in a camera shop or research on the internet before you buy.

Take all the film you think you will need—then add a couple of rolls. Film is not only hard to find in many places, it is also expensive.

Before you pack the film, stick a piece of tape on each roll and write consecutive numbers on them. Use the rolls in numerical order. Keep a record in your travel diary of your activities and what you photographed. Alongside the record, write the film's number.

When you take your film in to be developed, write each roll's number on the corresponding receipt from the top of the film developer's envelope.

After you get your pictures, match the receipts with the envelopes. Write the roll number from your receipts on the matching set of pictures.

With your travel diary and your pictures, you can make a memorable souvenir of your vacation.

Purse

A woman traveler's best friend is her purse. With it, you have the essentials you need every day.

▸ Facial tissue in small purse size packs can be used for toilet paper, towel, napkin or gift wrap. You never know which restroom won't have toilet paper; which restaurant will not provide napkins; which seat you want to sit on that will need dusting off; or which little souvenir will need protection in your pocket. Of course, tissues are always convenient for blowing your nose, too.

▸ Convert at least $200 into the local currency. Depending upon your destination, you can usually do that at a large bank before you go or at an airport exchange machine when you arrive. The money should be in coins and small denominational bills.

▸ Take no more than two credit cards. Be sure one of them can be used in an ATM. Check your limits before you go so you don't go over them. Take a copy of the cards and write the phone number and address of whom to call if they are lost or stolen.

▸ Reading material. I always carry a book in my purse and a couple more in my suitcase.

▸ Your passport. Carry it in a colorful envelope in a separate zippered compartment. I use vividly colored, nylon organizers with a velcro closing sold to carry store coupons. One source for them is: Hannah Hansen, 2901 W. Pico Blvd, Los Angeles, CA 90006. One organizer costs $6.94, two for $11.98 (includes P&H). Or, choose to carry your passport in a safety pouch around your neck and under your clothing.

▸ A currency converter. Preferably one with other data such as time differences, clothing sizes, duty-free imports, world currencies, distances, weights and measures. *(see the Resource Section for travel supply catalogs).*

▸ A small address book with the names and addresses of those to whom you will be mailing postcards, your insurance company, travel agent, doctor, embassy, etc.

NOTE: Check Chapter Ten for suggestions on buying a purse.

PURSE LIST

☐ Starred (*) items from grooming list
☐ Passport in envelope or pouch by itself
☐ Snack such as, apple, crackers, cheese (a must for persons with diabetes)
☐ Medication needed for the day
☐ Credit card/ATM. Only carry-one, keep the other in the hotel's or ship's safe.
☐ Money for the day in wallet
☐ ID in wallet
☐ Copy of itinerary
☐ Tickets, passes
☐ Insurance information
☐ Book
☐ Travel diary
☐ Address book
☐ Airmail postage stamps - theirs.
☐ Currency converter (see Resource Section)
☐ Glasses and sunglasses
☐ Artificial tears eye drops
☐ Breath mints
☐ Nail file
☐ Safety pins
☐ Travel pack of wet towelettes
☐ Hand lotion
☐ Film
☐ Closures for luggage. (Keep your home keys with your valuables in the hotel safe.)

Purse Organization

Carry a small, zippered bag in your purse for grooming supplies. The small bag makes the items easy to find and it is less likely to accidently open and make a mess.

Purchase two nylon envelopes with a velcro or zipper closure. On the zipper tab, fasten a small alligator clip. When you put the envelopes in your purse, clip them to the lining. They won't fall out and it is more difficult for someone to reach in and take them.

Tuck all your paper stuff in one envelope—receipts, stamps, address book, postcards, etc. In the other, keep your passport and visas, tickets, bus passes, keys, etc.

The envelopes keep like items together and eliminate clutter. The colors identify the contents easily.

Precautions

- Keep your purse zipped except when you are taking items in or out.
- Never hang your purse on the door hook of toilet compartments. Someone can reach over the door and be out of sight with it before you can give chase.
- Don't put your purse on the floor unless you put a foot through the handles. That way, no one can reach from behind you and steal it without your knowledge.
- Men can take their items with them in a waist-pack or small backpack. (*see travel supply companies in Resource Section.*)
- When walking on the street, stay away from the curb and carry your purse on the arm away from the street.

Chapter Thirteen

PACKING

Organize

- A month before your trip, organize your packing by placing three bins or boxes on the floor of your closet or room. Label one as suitcase, one as carry-on and one as purse. As you accumulate items, put them in the appropriate bin and check them off your lists.
- A week before your travel, you should have everything you plan to take all together.
- Clean and press (if necessary) all the clothes you plan to take with you. (Press and hang them a day or so ahead of time. Freshly pressed clothes may retain some moisture and will wrinkle easily.)
- Keep your appointments for hair and nails.
- See your doctor for a physical exam and fill your prescriptions.
- Meet with your contact person and go over all the details of your trip with them. Confirm what they are going to do for you while you are gone.
- Complete and check off the home safety list.
- Set aside what you will be wearing while you travel.

TIP: Choose comfortable clothing and shoes. Anything tight, scratchy or otherwise uncomfortable can make you feel miserable by the end of a long flight. Have a couple of layers of clothing so you can adjust to changes in temperature. When you are settled in your seat on the plane, slip off your shoes and put on your slipper socks.

- Two to three days before you leave, go over your lists to be sure you have everything. Then make two photocopies of the lists. Leave one with your contact person and take one with you. Then, in case of loss, you have an inventory of your belongings.
- Check your kitchen to be sure you have something you can fix to eat when you arrive home from your trip.
- The night before you leave, confirm your reservations and the times. Finish packing any last minute items. Close your suitcase and carry-on and place them by the door, ready for pickup.
- Get a good night's sleep but allow plenty of time for grooming, dressing and a last minute house check before your transportation to the airport arrives.

Last minute safety check

Check all the locks on house, windows, garages and storage buildings. Set your inside light monitors to go off and on in your usual pattern. Walk through with your safety check list to be sure everything is as it should be. Put your keys to the house in your purse. Leave the keys to the car at home.

Carry-on Packing List

- ☐ All items from medical list
- ☐ All items from first aid list
- ☐ Medication
- ☐ Items from grooming list
- ☐ A set of night clothes
- ☐ A change of clothing including underwear
- ☐ Camera
- ☐ Film in protective pouch
- ☐ Sewing (I take my counted cross-stitch to sew while I'm on a plane.)
- ☐ Documents from document list
- ☐ Insurance cards and emergency information
- ☐ Reading material
- ☐ Extra pair of glasses
- ☐ Replacement batteries for camera and any other items that need them. Keep in reclosable plastic bag
- ☐ An inflatable neck pillow
- ☐ Umbrella
- ☐ One or two 100 watt light bulbs

Packing Your Suitcase

Lay your open suitcase flat on the bed. Roll your underwear and socks. Stuff some of them into your shoes. Put your shoes in plastic bags or shoe bags to prevent scratches and keep them from soiling your clothes. Pack your shoes and books near the hinges of the suitcase so when it is closed the heaviest items will be on the bottom.

Button jackets. Place collar end next to the hinged edge. Fold the sleeves to the back and let remainder hang over the suitcase edge. Cushion the waist area with shirts or underwear, then fold the bottom of the jacket up into the upper sleeves.

Fold tee shirts and nightclothes, then roll. Button and fold blouses and shirts as they do in stores when they are new. You can place a roll of socks in the collar to maintain the shape.

Place stiff belts along the perimeter of the suitcase because rolling may cause them to crack.

Any toiletries or cosmetics you carry in your suitcase should be in reclosable plastic bags with the seal securely closed.

Pack sleepwear, or whatever you will need first, on top so you can reach it without ruffling through your carefully packed bag.

Pack the photo copies of your passport, airline tickets and itinerary,

Wrap jewelry in tissue, stow in a cloth bag or a rolled garment.

Pack your suitcase full but not stuffed. Both an under-packed and over-packed suitcase can cause wrinkling.

NOTE: If you are going on an exotic trip, such as a safari, the tour company and your travel agent can give you a list of any special items you may need. You can find most of these specialty items in travel stores.

When you arrive at your destination, unpack your suitcase and hang clothes that may wrinkle. To release unavoidable wrinkling, hang the garments in the bathroom, turn on the hot water, shut the door for a few minutes.

Save water! Take your shower at the same time.

Chapter Fourteen

RETURNING HOME

You have had a great vacation. A few glitches and some disappointments but all in all, you had fun. Then why are you sitting in your living room feeling blue?

Not to worry, this is a normal thing. After the long planning time, the excited anticipation and then the trip itself, coming home is anticlimactic.

The degree to which you suffer the post-vacation blues relates to four factors:

1. **Personality factors** can contribute to disappointment and depression. Perhaps your expectations were too high. Did you say to yourself, "This must be a perfect trip." Humans and their lives are *never* perfect, so having unrealistic ideas may cause you to be disappointed a lot. Drop your irrational idea of perfection and make a list of the enjoyable experiences on your trip.

   Maybe you were angry or depressed before you left but suppressed your feelings because you wanted to have fun on your vacation. These feelings do not go away without some sort of resolution. Now, in the aftermath of the travel, they surface again with a vengeance.

   The first step in getting rid of these feelings is to recognize they exist and that you can do something about them. It is important you don't tell yourself the vacation caused the feelings.

Other personality factors such as, needing to be in control, trouble-making "frenemies," and trouble adjusting quickly to new environments may contribute to the post-vacation blues. Look at the factors honestly and assess how much they effect you.

2. **Your job** can contribute to post-vacation blues. If you hated your job before you left, you will not be happy to get back to it. Maybe you are the only one in your position and you know piles of work are waiting for you. Conversely, if you felt your fellow workers could not get along without you and they did fine, you may be unhappy and even confused.

3. **How well you planned your vacation** is a big factor. If you followed the planning suggestions in this book, the chances are you will be returning with good feelings about your vacation. A lackadaisical "We'll figure out what to do when we get there" will usually lead to time-consuming glitches that could have been avoided.

4. **Attitudes** based on irrational thinking such as "Everything must go perfectly or my trip is ruined" will result in unhappiness. Nothing goes perfectly on a vacation. Relax and deal with problems as they occur. Most problems are only vacation ruining when you allow them to be. Tell yourself, "I don't like this situation but it can ruin my trip only if I let it."

Of course, major disasters can occur but they happen infrequently. Your extensive preplanning made provision for most of them.

Your body may experience physical changes during travel

that can cause uneasy feelings when it is over. At the end of a good vacation your pulse and your breathing may be slowed. When you get back to your normal routine your body may feel out of sync until you get up to speed again. The process may take a few days. Relax and don't worry about it and you will be able to handle it better.

If you can, take a couple of post-vacation days off. Don't rush around. Do everything at a moderate pace. Allow yourself time to daydream about the trip. Relive the pleasurable parts of it.

The next day, pick up your pace. Begin to unpack, wash clothes, shop for groceries, pick up your mail and prepare yourself to go back into your normal routines.

TIP: Before you leave, be sure your home is clean and orderly. Have some staples on hand so you can fix a simple meal or a cup of coffee without running to the store the day you get home.

Call to have your paper restarted, your phone off call-forwarding, etc. Call friends and relatives.

Take your pictures in for developing. Remember to stick the number from your film canister on each receipt. When you pick them up, match the numbers on the receipts with the envelopes. Place them in an album with the comments from your travel diary. Paste in other souvenirs you found such as, menus or napkins, postcards, stickers, and maybe a flower or plant that intrigued you. Relax and enjoy making this memorable record of your vacation.

Later, look at any problems you had while traveling. Honestly assess what happened. Could you have prevented it by more careful planning, more alertness to your surroundings or other factors within your control? What could you have done differently?

Realize that unplanned things happen. If you could have planned better, resolve to do that next time. If not, let it go.

Events can only continue to bother you if you catastrophize and ruminate over them. Say to yourself, "I wish that hadn't happened but it did but now it's over and I will let it go."

Note From the Author

My goal when writing this book was and is to make your travel easier and more pleasurable. Please e-mail your comments, ideas and suggestions. I would love to hear from you.

E-mail: joyn0429@sbcglobal.net

The End.

RESOURCE SECTION

Canada Information
Detailed information for travelers to Canada including entry into the country.
http://gocanada.

Currency Convertor
Search for "currency converter" on the internet for multiple companies offering free conversions. *Www.magellans.com* has a hand-held size, battery operated combination currency converter/calculator for $6.95. Catalog number CC151

Federal Citizen Information Center
Offers hundreds of consumer orinted publications for free or at minimal cost. Order a free copy of the *2004 Consumer Action Handbook* and a catalog from:
FCIC-Consumer Action Handbook
PO Box 100
Pueblo CO 81002
Or call: 888-878-3256
You can also access a version of the handbook and see other available publications at: *www.consumeraction.gov*

Health
▸ **Asthma and Allergy Foundation of America**
1233 20th Street NW
Washington DC 20030
202-466–7643
www.aafa.org

- **Center for Disease Control**
  www.cdc.gov or call
  Travelers Health Information: 877-394-8747
  Immunization Hotline: 800-232-2522
  General Information: 800-311-3435

- **The Diabetic Traveler** (quarterly newsletter)
  $18.95 per year
  The Diabetic Traveler
  PO Box 8223 RW
  Stamford CT 06905
  Subscription includes a free business card sized insulin adjustment guide for air travel through multiple time zones and 4 page article "Management of Diabetes During Intercontinental Travel."

- **IAMAT—International Association for Medical Assistance to Travelers**
  417 Center Street
  Lewiston, NY 14092
  716-754-4883
  www.iamat.org
  A wonderful service for travelers. There is no charge to join but they do ask for a donation to support the organization's work. They send you a membership card entitling you to a world directory of participating physicians in 550 countries and territories. All doctors have been screened and were trained in an English-speaking country. IAMAT doctors have agreed to specific fees for office or hotel visits. Weekends and holidays cost $10 more.

  With membership, you also receive a passport sized record for your medical history, a world immunization chart, and other printed material including the sanitary conditions of food, milk and water, and information about malaria.

- **Medic-Alert**
  2323 Colorado Avenue
  Turlock CA 95382
  800-432-5378
  www.medicalert.org
  This company sells bracelets and necklaces to alert people to your severe allergies, diabetes or any other chronic medical condition. The bracelet or necklace has an engraved panel with your allergy information and a 24-hour emergency number that doctors or paramedics can call for more details about your medical condition. The cost is $35 for the first year. This includes the basic metal, engraved panel. Other metals and designs are available and the cost is higher. Each subsequent year there will be a $15 annual membership fee to keep your medical information updated and on record.

- **Medicool, Inc**
  23520 Telo Avenue, # 6
  Torrance CA 90505
  800-433-2469
  www.medicool.com
  Travel kits for diabetics. Includes cooling pack for insulin.

- **Prevention Magazine**
  www.prevention.com
  800-813-8070
  Search for health tips for travelers

Hostels

- **Elderhostel**
  PO Box 1959
  Wakefield, MA 01180
  Toll-free Phone: 877-426-8056
  www.elderhostel.org
  Educational travel for mature travelers.

- **Hostelling International**
Membership information: Forsyth Travel Library, Inc, 9154 West 57th St., Shawnee Mission, KS 66201. Call 800-367-7984. Inexpensive travel for all ages.

Insurance

http://InsureMyTrip.com bills itself as "The Travel Insurance Comparison Site" You can get quotes from numerous travel insurance companies, compare exactly what features they offer, and their prices. You can also check the A.M. Best ratings for each company to be sure you are buying from a financially stable insurer.

Mexico Online

Detailed information for visitors to Mexico including driving into Mexico.
www.mexonline.com

Road Safety

- **Travel Reports**
Issued by the Association for Safe International Road Travel. These reports describe driving conditions in 95+ countries.
www..asirt.org or call 301-983-5252

Safari Travel Tips

- *www.africansafaritravel.com*
Articles and information on safaris
- www.gotoafrica.com/home_safari/default.asp
Searchable database of safaris with featured destinations
- *www. onsafari.com*
Articles and tips on safari destinations

Train Travel

▸ **RailEurope Group (includes BritRail)**
Westchester One
44 South Broadway, 11th floor
White Plains NY 10601
1-800-4-EURAIL
www. raileurope.com

Travel Consultants

▸ *www.astanet.com*
Home page of the American Society of Travel Agents
▸ *www.ntaonline.com*
Home page of the National Tour Association
▸ *www.ustoa.com*
Home page of the United States Tour Operators Association

Travel Supply Companies

▸ **Corporate Travel Safety**
437 Park Fortuna
Calabasas CA 91302-1714
www.corporatesafety.com
Waist bags with special safety features and other travel supplies

▸ **Damart**
3 Front Street
Rollinsford NH 03805
800-258-7300
Fax: 1-603-742-2050
www.damart.com
Call or check website to order free catalog of warm, lightweight garments including thermal underwear.

▸ **Long Road Travel Supplies**
111 Avenida Drive
Berkeley CA 94709
800-359-6040

159

www.longroad.com
Mosquito nets and other travel accessories

▸ **Magellan's Travel Company**
110 W. Sola Street
Santa Barbara, CA 93101-3007
800-962-4943
Fax: 800-962-4940
www.magellans.com
Call for catalog. Sells travel equipment, luggage, travel books, safety items and other accessories.

▸ **TravelSmith**
60 Leveroni Court
Novato CA 94949
800-950-1600 (Catalog and orders)
www.travelsmith.com
A large assortment of easy-care travel clothes and luggage for men and women

U.S. Customs Service

The Customs Service is improving its customer service to international travelers at major U.S. travel hubs by having passenger service reps available to travelers at more than 20 international airports and some seaports where cruise ships dock. Their major purpose is to help travelers clear customs.

The second new service is automated booths or kiosks. All the traveler has to do is type in their country of destination on the self-service computer with a touch screen display and the computer will print the information for you. The screen displays a phone number to call for more information

Customs kiosks are located in the outbound passenger lounges at the following international airports: Atlanta, Boston, Charlotte in NC, Chicago, Dallas/Ft. Worth, Detroit, Houston, JFK in New York, Los Angeles, Miami, Newark in NJ,

Philadelphia, San Francisco, San Juan, and Washington/Dulles.
More are planned.
U.S. Customs Service
1300 Pennsylvania Ave NW
Washington, DC 20229
www.customs.gov

▸ **Know Before You Go**
Booklet from U.S. Customs with customs hints for returning
residents. Order from internet site or U.S. Customs Service, 1301
Constitution Avenue NW, Washington D.C. 20229

U.S. Government Resources

▸ **Consular Information Sheets, Travel Warnings and Public
Announcements** may be heard anytime by dialing 202-647-5225
from a touch tone phone or get detailed information from their
website at:
http://travel.state.gov/travel_warnings.html

▸ **U.S. State Department, Consular Affairs Publications**
Available for sale from the Superintendent of Documents, U.S.
Government Printing Office, Washington DC 20402. Phone 202-
512-1800 for prices and availability.
A small sample of the publications offered include:

✓ *A Safe Trip Abroad* contains helpful precautions one can take
to minimize the chance of becoming a victim of terrorism or
crime.

✓ *Travel Tips for Older Americans* Contains special health,
safety and travel information for older Americans.

✓ *Your Trip Abroad* offers tips on obtaining a passport,
considerations in preparing for your trip, and other sources of
information.

▶ **Backgound Notes** are brief, factual pamphlets describing the countries of the world. They contain current information on each country's people, culture, geography, history, government, economy, and political conditions. Single copies may be ordered from the U.S. Government Printing Office, Washington DC. You can also order *Background Notes* on the internet site at: *http://www.state.gov/www/background_notes/index.html*

▶ **Overseas assistance for U. S. Citizens**
When you travel independently, you can get help from American Embassies and Consulates; the Overseas Citizen Services or American Express (members only).

Overseas Citizen Services deals with emergencies involving individual Americans abroad—death, sickness, destitution, accidents or arrest. Working with embassies and consulates, the center is the link between the citizens in distress and their families in the U.S. When calling from the United States, their phone number is 888-407-4747, twenty-four hours a day, seven days a week. If you call from overseas, the phone number is 317-472-2328.

Note: Other publications are available from the GPO. See www.travel.state.gov

162

BOOK LIST

Bundren, Mary Rodgers. *Travel Wise With Children: 101 Educational Travel Tips for Families.* Imprint Publishing, Inc. 1998. Price $12.95. Order from Bookworld: 800-444-2524 or *www.bookworld.com* and Amazon.com

Davidson, Nadine Nardi. *Travel With Others Without Wishing They'd Stayed Home.* Prince Publishing. 1999. Available at bookstores and Amazon.com. Price $16.95
How to choose a compatible travel companion

Kruger, Davida F. *The Diabetes Travel Guide.* Order from the American Diabetes Association. Call 800-232-6733 or go to their web site at *http://store.diabetes.org* (www not needed for this address.) $14.95
Detailed information on all aspects of diabetes for travelers.

Nolting, Mark. *African Safari Journal.* Order from Global Travel Publishers, 5353 N. Federal Highway, Ste 300, Ft. Lauderdale FL 33308 and Amazon.com Call: 800-882-9453. Fax: 954-781-0984. E-mail: noltinggaac@aol.com. $16.95
Where to go, climate, planning, clothes and more

Meyers, Carole Terwilliger. *101 Great Car Games & Activities* (for children 4 +) Order from: Carousel Press, PO Box 6038, Berkeley CA 94706. Price $8.95

Travel Publishers Association has many publishers of travel related books as its members. Their catalog is online at www.travelpubs@ginkgopress.com. The association is managed by Joan Peterson, the author of the Eat Smart books.

INDEX

170

Printed in the United States
26708LVS00002B/81